SHIN Sang-ok

Korean Film Directors

The Korean Film Directors series is one of Korean Film Council's projects to furnish an international audience with insight and analysis into the works of Korea's most representative film directors.

The series aims to expand upon the existing body of knowledge on Korean film, educate the general public of the history of Korean film and Korean film directors, and draw attention to the significance of works that represent Korean film. Critics who share their insight in the series are leaders in their respective specialties. Each volume includes critical commentary on films, an extensive interview with the director, and a comprehensive filmography for reference.

SHIN Sang-ok

Written by YI Hyo-in
Translated by Colin A. Mouat

SHIN Sang-ok
Written by YI Hyo-in

Korean Film Council
206-46 Cheongnyangni-dong, Dongdaemun-gu, Seoul 130-010, Korea
Phone (82-2) 9587-596
Fax (82-2) 9587-590
http://www.kofic.or.kr/english
email: pdh21@kofic.or.kr

Published by **Seoul Selection**
B1 Korean Publishers Association Bldg., 105-2 Sagan-dong, Jongno-gu, Seoul 110-190, Korea
Phone (82-2) 734-9567
Fax (82-2) 734-9562
http://www.seoulselection.com
email: pubco@seoulselection.com

ISBN: 978-89-91913-43-1 03680

Printed in the Republic of Korea

Contents

Preface

When I was young, at a time when we might learn the names of novelists or poets but never that of a film director, the first name I learned may have been that of SHIN Sang-ok. After that, I learned the name of KIM Hyo-cheon (who had the same first name as my older brother), and then I think I came to recognize HA Kil-jong and LEE Chang-ho as directors. And then, after some time, the names of countless Korean and foreign directors came into my head, yet even then SHIN Sang-ok was somehow unfamiliar. The reason for this was that, at the time when I was busily learning the names of directors, SHIN was in North Korea. Political taboos were so rife at the time that I recall lowering my voice a little and looking around me whenever I talked about SHIN Sang-ok with my friends in film. In that way, he came to stay with me as an even more mythical figure. Actually, there was nowhere to see his films at that time, so virtually the only images of him that remained with me were certain scenes from his film *Eunuch*, which I saw when I was a child, and a few scenes from *Red Muffler*.

Around the time when I was studying Korean film history and beginning to work as a film critic, I always tended to avoid facing up to the inscrutable figure of SHIN Sang-ok. It may have been because I couldn't re-watch most of the films he had made, and because I wasn't sure how I should look at him following his escape from North Korea. However, at some point I was assessing films made by SHIN's teachers and students, and I had the opportunity to see the films he had made in North Korea and just a small portion of the films he had made before being kidnapped. In the process, I think I became able to put forth a provisional assessment on him.

But now, as I put out this book, I have come to think that I should modify the assessment that I made. Not only have I gained a new sense on his cinematic and historical views, but I have also come to the conclusion that it may be possible to view many aspects of Korean film history in a new light or reinterpret them through a study of SHIN Sang-ok. In addition, I tried to avoid viewing SHIN as one director who made certain cinematic texts, since it appeared as though he had made his films while surrounded by a system he had constructed himself. But this does not mean that I want to say that it is not possible to find any personal originality or authorial characteristics, let alone that this book represents some grand discovery or the recounting of something shrouded in secrecy. I have done my utmost to dissolve such feelings and judgments within the words of the book, and I have also come to the conclusion that I should do further research in the future.

This book is made up of the following parts: "SHIN Sang-ok, Another History," which falls under the area of a discussion of the director; "SHIN Sang-ok and the SHIN Sang-ok System," wherein I attempt to examine SHIN's cinematic and social activities from various angles; excerpted portions of interviews conducted by the film researcher LEE Gi-rim for the magazine *Cine 21*; a personal biography and chronological record of his works; and a list of synopses. As SHIN is no longer with us, no new interview was possible, and after examining several interviews I decided to print LEE Gi-rim's, since it seemed the most appropriate for this book. I extend my thanks to her. Also, though I was unable to include it separately, I extend my thanks to EBS producer AHN Tae-geun, who graciously allowed me consult interviews that he had conducted.

July 2008
YI Hyo-in

On the Director

SHIN Sang-ok, Another History

Master

SHIN Sang-ok directed 74 films during the 52 years from his debut with 1952's *The Evil Night* to his final film, 2004's unreleased *A Winter Story*. This includes films that he made in North Korea and the United States. This number of works cannot be called very large when viewed against the period of his activity. In comparison with prolific directors like IM Kwon-taek, KIM Soo-yong, or Japan's Kinoshita Keisuke, he could be said to have made relatively few films. But the period in which his major works were produced was generally restricted to the 1960s. Also, he is not represented by one sole work, as YU Hyun-mok is with *Aimless Bullet* (1961) or KIM Ki-young is with *The Housemaid* (1960). This may be because his major works, while outstanding, do not have that "certain clear something" that crosses cinema and art history, and it may be because of his tendency toward diverse works that combined films of diverse genres.

KIM Su-nam writes: "In 1975, the Japanese film magazine *Kinema Junbo* selected and printed a list of major foreign directors representing world cinema for its supplementary edition (December, Vol. 21), and SHIN was the only Korean director included on this list of world directors. The cinematic author was introduced in the journal as a director of the social school who frankly portrayed the reality of Korea within various political constraints."[1] It appears that perhaps he was called a "social school" director in consideration of the revocation of the registration for his film company Shin Films. But if he is referred to as a director from the social school, this ends up offering a somewhat narrow selection or imprecise designation, as he not only made films in various different genres, he also made films with a strong scent of collaboration with national policy.

KIM Su-nam, perhaps finding it difficult to define a director who made films with such diverse inclinations as SHIN Sang-ok with a single word, referred to him as a "master of mise-en-scène."[2] It is certainly undeniable that SHIN's films had particularly beautiful mise-en-scène in comparison with other Korean films of the time. In his *Deaf Samryong-i*, the image of Samryong and his master's wife crossing the village where the river flows is reminiscent of Eastern painting, and in the scene of the whole village, captured in a long shot, as Samryong fetches the village's doctor of Korean medicine, the characters' movements are comic yet dynamically linked, allowing the audience to be drawn into the urgency of their emotions. An obvious analysis would be that SHIN Sang-ok was familiar with the composition of mise-en-scène because of his history as an art major, but one cannot help noting that he also had his

Deaf Samryong-i, 1964

1. KIM Su-nam, *Korean Director Theory 2*, Jisik Saneopsa, 2003, pp. 115-116.
2. Ibid., p. 115.

own outstanding sense for connecting the narrative and image. However, in explaining SHIN Sang-ok the director, it would be difficult to reach a consensus on treating "mise-en-scène" as the most important element. To explain his films, it is also necessary to explain various other elements.

SHIN said the following: "The greatest weakness in my films, as I see it, is that they lack the thick scent of life and a vivid reality. This is my frank confession. I became famous unexpectedly at a young age, and since then I've been so deeply into film that I haven't had a moment to look anywhere else. As a result, I haven't had the luxury of having a diverse range of experience and sensing and thinking about the depth of life, and I've always used haste as an excuse for not allowing each of my films to mature properly so that a deep flavor can emerge."[3] This passage comes from the first part of SHIN's autobiography. But it is impossible to accept unquestioningly the verdict laid down by a veteran director in his final years as he ruminated over his life. His words may be correct if the standard used is "perfection," but it cannot be said of his films that they lacked the scent of life and a vivid reality in comparison with other films of the time. In the chapter of this book entitled "SHIN Sang-ok and the SHIN Sang-ok System," there is a quote from SHIN, in a conversation with the novelist CHOE In-ho, saying something along the lines of how he thought it would be OK for him and other directors like KIM Ki-young and YU Hyun-mok to leave the profession. It seems reasonable to interpret the above quote in this context as well.

In this writer's view, the most appropriate designation for SHIN Sang-ok might be "the most artistically skilled master." It is possible to say this first of all because SHIN Sang-ok made the greatest works of the time in every genre, whether historical drama, melodrama, period comedy, war film, didactic melodrama or literary adaptation. Second, SHIN used the most advanced technology available at the time in Korea, and led the Korean film world as both a director and a technician. The third point is an external element to his films, but through his company Shin Films, he provided countless directors with the opportunity to make

3. SHIN Sang-ok, *I, Was Film*, Random House Korea, 2007, p. 21.

films or otherwise accounted for a large portion of Korean film history through his leadership. To him, film seems to have been a "goal in itself" that went beyond a mere expedient or means of making a living. Otherwise, he would not have been able to rise to the position of emperor of Korean film by his early 30s and assume a place as a major figure in Korean cinema for close to twenty years.

SHIN Sang-ok

KIM Ki-young

YU Hyun-mok

Escape from Poverty

"It may help to think of film as to some extent creating a human community or ideal society to escape from the intolerance, constraints and cruelty of real society, development and despotism. In short, there is always a desire for Utopia within the ideas of directors."[4] Under this premise, Jacques Aumont categorized Rainer Werner Fassbinder as having pursued "films to help in living," Andrei Tarkovsky as having aimed at "art for everyone" and Godard as having achieved "retreat as salvation." Then what (cinematic) ideological starting point is there for SHIN Sang-ok? The answer is the escape from poverty. SHIN wrote, "It was a time of refuge, when everyone was suffering, and our home too was one where the whole family had to cluster together in one narrow room. It was terribly uncomfortable screening off the middle of the room with a blanket every night and

4. Jacques Aumont, *Les Théories des Cinéaste* (Korean trans.), Dongmunseon, 2005, p. 205.

trying to sleep together with my mother, my older brother and his wife. So I would always walk around outside, and one day I met a *yangbuin* (a prostitute who catered to foreigners) and lived with her for about six months. That experience contributed quite a bit to *The Evil Night*."[5] Nowadays the print of *The Evil Night* has been lost and the film can no longer be seen, but I have heard that the film includes on its soundtrack George Gershwin's "Rhapsody in Blue." A poor artist, unable to pay the rent and on the verge of eviction, goes out in search of money but is unable to find any. He is on his way back after a night of heavy drinking with a friend when he is struck by a car. In the car is a *yangbuin*, and he ends up staying at her house. This is the film's story, and if there is any ideology behind the film, it is the "escape from poverty." In order to allow the escape from poverty, it is natural that proper social systems should exist guaranteeing stable production, and fair distribution must also be realized. As the whole of society was poor, and he himself was poor, the early films that SHIN made always carry the looming shadow of the problem of poverty. In *The Evil Night*, the main character is leaving after spending the night at the prostitute's house when he runs into his wife, who coincidentally has found a new apartment next door to the prostitute. The film ends as he flies into a blind rage and drags his bicycle cart on to parts unknown.[6] This is not a story that is tied up in blind passion. It is an elegy in which nightmarish days have followed one after the other, and where more are predicted to continue into the future.

Following his debut with *The Evil Night*, SHIN worked as a successful rookie director with *A College Woman's Confession* (1958), and at this time in Korean society, the problem of surviving in the devastation following the war was regarded as the most important issue. However, this did not mean that the young people of Korea were focusing only on that problem. According to OH Yeong-suk, "Seoul at that time was a street of ruins, where everything was destroyed, factories and urban districts alike. Naturally, there were no jobs, and the streets were filled with the unemployed. The poet GO Eun recalls that the main professions of citizens of

5. SHIN Sang-ok, 2007, p. 49.
6. The outline of this film is also from SHIN's book cited above, pp. 47 and 48.

Seoul at that time were A-frame carrier, rag picker and prostitute [...] As historians have recently revealed, the 1950s may have been an age of ruins, but at the same time it was also an age of a "great outpouring of energy," where people were searching within it for a new beginning."[7] Even amid the ruins, there remain a firm determination toward reconstruction and a curiosity about sex, the body and culture. Just like in Japan, which had been occupied at that time by the American army and only became an independent state in 1952, the desire for restoration and curiosity about sex and culture would not have escaped joining the issue of survival as popular interests in Korean society as well. In *Stray Dog*, made by the Japanese master Akira Kurosawa in 1949, the characters of a pickpocket and detective whose gun is stolen appear, and both men share the common experience of having lost their backpacks on the way home after the war's end. This film also contains a city in ruins and houses like mud huts, but amid all of that there is also the vitality of a baseball stadium swarming with 50,000 spectators and the vigorous dancing of the girls at a dance hall. The film's conclusion sees the captured pickpocket letting out an animalistic wail and weeping, but the sound is drowned out by the noises of a piano coming from some nearby house and the singing of children. The meaning of this is that human vitality is showing through even amid ruins and disorder, and that things are being brought into order as people move toward a new society. But this is not what is portrayed in *The Evil Night*—all the more so as it was the middle of a war.

By 1955, however, it appeared that Korea as well had entered that kind of a mood. LEE Gyu-hwan's *Story of Chun-hyang* (1955) was a big hit at the box office, and HAN Hyeong-mo's *Madame Freedom* (1955), which depicted a married woman going astray, had many people talking. SHIN made *Korea*(1954), a semi-documentary introducing the nation, and then followed it with *Dreams* (1955), based on a novel by LEE Kwang-su, one of the major modern authors working in Korea, and with *The Youth* (1955), which depicted the feuding of political enemies, centering on Prince Daewon, the father of the last Joseon King

7. OH Yeong-suk, *1950s Korean Film and Cultural Discourse*, Somyeong Publishing, 2007, pp. 16-17.

Gojong, who stepped down after serving as regent. *The Youth* was also based on a novel, this one by KIM Dong-in, who was one of the twin pillars of Korean modern literature along with LEE Kwang-su.

SHIN recalled, "It was exceedingly natural and obvious that I would make films with this kind of tendency. Film is fundamentally an endeavor of searching for beauty and creating dreams. Ever since I studied art, aesthetic elements assumed a large place within my consciousness."[8] The director's explanation of the background for the creation of these films provides a clue toward understanding them. When he mentions "this kind of tendency," he is referring to the so-called "literary film" based on a novel that has already been evaluated positively. *Dreams* tells the story of a young Buddhist monk who falls in love with the daughter of an aristocrat and has a passionate romance with her, until in the end it is revealed that

Dreams, 1955

8. SHIN Sang-ok, 2007, p. 57.

it was all dreams; the film contains an Eastern philosophy where life and dreams are difficult to tell apart. If one views it only in terms of this one film, it appears that what SHIN Sang-ok was pursuing in 1955 was neither ideology nor reality, but aesthetic cinematic expression. *The Youth* as well is a film about the confrontation between families, not a collectivist work dealing with the story of the rage and vengeance of a people whose country has been taken away from them. Here, the issue is not a question of historical right and wrong. SHIN always remained a step back from problems at the group level, for example that of the people or the state.

SHIN Sang-ok was a so-called "displaced person" who had lived in North Korea before moving South. The displaced had to live in an unfamiliar place, and thus are often depicted as tenacious and stubborn people. Also, because they came to the South because they disliked the communist government in the North, they typically are ideologically to the right or clearly opposed to the communist government. It is not easy to say anything clear about what kind of ideology SHIN Sang-ok possessed politically, but it does at least appear that he was not someone opposed to the dominant ideology in South Korean society. This is expressed in his book as well: "I am a cinematically single-minded type who thinks only of film, but I have always thought that the cinematic artists of a developing country have an obligation to contribute to reality about 30% of the time, and even now I have not changed in this conviction. Film is not simple entertainment. In a film, there must a righteous truth that transcends what is merely interesting, whether it is human victory, justice or the natural movement of all things toward the right path."[9] But SHIN's "30% doctrine of reality contribution" becomes a valid logic only when based upon an acknowledgement of the legitimacy and public nature of the political administration. If this is the case, then the making of *Evergreen Tree* (1961) and *Rice* (1963) can be seen as the result of SHIN's positive view of the PARK Chung-hee administration as well as the practical application of his "30% doctrine." Among South Koreans, opinions for and against PARK Chung-hee are

9. Ibid., p. 77.

extremely divergent. People who note the period's economic growth and PARK's strong leadership praise the man, while people who note his suppression of human rights, the deepening of economic subordination to outside powers and the destruction of the traditional way of life that occurred under his administration criticize him. In SHIN's case, it appears that the director's view was one of general agreement, if not active agreement.

Evergreen Tree chronicles the struggles of passionate young men and women fighting to awaken an agricultural village economically and educationally while resisting the Japanese occupation. What is important here are not the aspects of direct struggle against the Japanese, but the parts about enlightening the villagers. SHIN based his film on a novel by SHIM Hoon, with no direct connection to PARK Chung-hee. Essentially, SHIN had realized his own spirit of times during his period of poverty. It appears that this was unrelated to any ideology he himself possessed or any judgment of the government. But at the time of the making of *Rice*, he had come to meet PARK Chung-hee following *Evergreen Tree*, and the two became somewhat close, with showings of SHIN's films at the Blue House every time he released one, so that it appears that some unspoken ideological exchange took place between them. This was not any grandiose ideology, but the simple ideology of "development and growth for their own sake," with the "issue of surviving" regarded as most important. *Rice* is based on the true story of the creation of fertile agricultural land through the boring of a tunnel through a mountain to bring water to a poor country village. The conclusion of the film, where they overcome the objections of landowners to the tunnel project and ultimately succeed, is accomplished with the help of the government. But even this, SHIN wrote, "was my intention at the time, and not anything anybody forced upon me."[10] To him, political or ideological inclinations were not the main thing; it was merely cinematic expression within the limitations imposed upon him, based on the current or spirit of the times.

The central characters in *Evergreen Tree* and *Rice* are not ideological figures,

10. Ibid., p. 79.

but individuals who devote themselves to a personal mission for the sake of the community. They are simply sincere people who do their best individually with indomitable will, but at the same time they are also people who never question their own beliefs. The strength of this class of film by SHIN Sang-ok comes thanks to the establishment of characters such as these, and their great welcome by audiences at the time likely also originated from this aspect. If, on the other hand, the films come across as naive, this too is due to the appearance of such "characters with strong convictions." But, ignoring all of these things, what is more evident is that SHIN's theme is the "escape from poverty." The dismal mood of *The Evil Night*, which foresaw the continuation of poverty, had transformed with the passage of 10 years into a posture confident enough to speak of a new construction.

Privatized History

In Japan during the 1970s and 1980s, yearlong miniseries were shown on NHK every Sunday in one-hour installments, and one of the constantly recurring genres was the *Chûshinkura* (忠臣藏). In these stories, 47 *rônin*, samurais who have lost their masters with the fall of Japan's solitary feudal lords following the unification of the Japanese government, fight to avenge their masters, who have committed ritual suicide by seppuku due to a law that the *rônin* view as mistaken. The stories were televised many times with different writers and also became a genre of Japanese film as well. At the time, the popularity of the *Chûshinkura* shown on TV was said to be linked with a spirit of the times among the Japanese that prioritized "the organization over the individual."[11] Thus, it could be called an example of period pieces and historical dramas being used actively to bind the people together as one or to mobilize them under a certain banner. It meant that film could be used as the means of a national mobilization system, so to speak. Several films about the general YI Sun-sin, who repelled the Japanese fleet during the Joseon Era, were produced under the PARK Chung-hee military administration, and these films correspond precisely to such examples.

Let us examine the historical dramas and period pieces of SHIN Sang-ok with this in mind.

First, there are films that deal with the period of political upheaval in the late Joseon Dynasty or with political subject matter, including *The Youth* (1955) and *LEE Seung-man and the Independence Movement* (1959); *Prince Daewon* (1968), which portrays a figure who enjoyed authority as the father of the late Joseon king before being driven out; and *The Three-Day Reign* (1973), which depicts an incident where passionate youths, following along with the Japanese Meiji Restoration, attempted to set up a modern government with Japanese support only to meet with failure. Among these films, *The Three-Day Reign* gives the sense of an attitude far removed from the director's spirit of the times. The director himself

11. Tsurumi Shunsuke, *The Popular Culture of Postwar Japan* (Korean trans.), Hallym Sinseo, 1996, pp. 128-129.

recalled, "[*LEE Seung-man and the Independence Movement*] was made through the forced mobilization of the entire cinema world for the promotion of President RHEE Syngman (aka LEE Seung-man), who ran for president in the latter days of the Liberal Party. The anti-communist youth league of IM Hwa-su, famous for political thuggery, was in charge of the production, and GWAK Yeong-ju, the Chief Bodyguard at the Blue House, was providing support from behind the scenes [...] It was a truly sad time, with the actor KIM Hui-gap having to go into the hospital with a broken rib after being hit by IM Hwa-su. But in my case, I didn't feel any sense of coercion. I put the film that I had been shooting on hold and went to make it, so you could say that I was essentially dragged there, but I wasn't forced to do anything I didn't want to do. It was subject matter that I had wanted to try and the production conditions were optimal as well."[12] Unlike the case of PARK Chung-hee, as discussed before, more Koreans probably hold feelings of opposition toward RHEE Syngman rather than agreement, so much so that his historical assessment could be called controversial, as he was forced from office through citizen demonstrations. Yet SHIN Sang-ok viewed it as an opportunity to maximize his own cinematic expression and took on the project with pleasure. The three films share the point that they always view Japan as threatening. The title character in *Prince Daewon* is ousted by the Japanese Empire, and KIM Ok-gyun in *The Three-Day Reign* cooperates with the Japanese for the sake of his own ambitions, but is ultimately abandoned, while RHEE Syngman is a figure who fights against the Japanese, if only for a short time.

Second, there are historical dramas set in past eras, including *Pagoda of No Shadows* (1957), which tells a story about the love of legendary characters who built a tower during the Silla Period; *SEONG Chun-hyang* (1961), which adapted a Korean traditional novel and was a phenomenal hit; *Madam White Snake* (1960), which told the odd tale of a white snake that turns into a human and has a romance; *A Reluctant Prince* (1963), the story of a king who became the scapegoat in the political infighting of high-ranking officials; *King Cheoljong and Bongnyeo*

12. SHIN Sang-ok, 2007, pp. 64-65.

(1963), and *Eunuch* (1968), which tells of an illicit palace affair involving a palace eunuch. It does not appear that SHIN viewed it as particularly important to interpret history justly or to interpret it from anyone's side. The historical incidents that he mainly selected, centering on periods of rapid upheaval, may have been merely texts in which he read artistic interest or the internal workings of people.

Third, there are his most famous works, the films that best show his method of reading history, including *Prince Yeonsan* (1961) and *Yeonsan the Tyrant*, which told the story of the man known as the biggest tyrant in the Joseon Era. First, this is what SHIN himself had to say: "The reason why I made a relatively large amount of historical dramas was partially because I have a lot of interest in history, but more than that because it was a means of telling the story that I wanted to tell while avoiding censorship."[13] What could he have meant by "the story that he wanted to tell while avoiding censorship"? To understand this, let us listen to some of his other words: "*LEE Seung-man and the Independence Movement* instilled in me the possibilities of and confidence in a film at a large scale. Also, it got me interested in modern Korean history, from the late Joseon Period to the formation of the Republic of Korea. That was a great gain for me. If you connect films I made in my later period, including *A Reluctant Prince*, *King Cheoljong and Bongnyeo*, *Prince Daewon*, *The Sino-Japanese War and the Heroic Queen Min*, *The Three-Day Reign* and *LEE Seung-man and the Independence Movement*, you can probably grasp my historical consciousness to some extent." If these films are connected (though they have not all survived and some must be compared only in terms of the surviving records), one can discern the common trait of the main characters in the films in that they are all figures who have failed politically. Thus, they share the common characteristic of having been represented by a political group that pursued some righteous cause or benefit within the greater trends of history before being unfortunately dragged down. In SHIN's eyes, the individual and the group, or individual ambition and political currents, could never join hands.

13. Ibid., p. 82
14. Ibid., p. 66

Before coming to any judgment about what story he wanted to tell with *Prince Yeonsan*, let us first critique the film by substituting human suffering for historical fact and interpreting it from the perspective of the mending of a wounded patriarchy. "You could take the point where I diverge from the source by placing the death of JANG Nok-su at the point where the internal conflict of Yeonsan is at its highest, placing the responsibility for his tyranny on her. Through the role-play in which he places JANG Nok-su on his throne as himself and castigates the king's (JANG Nok-su's) mistakes from the perspective of one of his subjects (Yeonsan), the king looks back on his own sins and eliminates JANG Nok-su, who symbolizes palace intrigue and his own lust for power."[15] Thus, after Yeonsan erases his own faults by chastising JANG Nok-su, he is saved once again by Madame SHIN, his virtuous wife, who comforts him by saying, "Your Majesty acted badly, but we at least know that you are not a bad person. That which was bad and wrong was due to conventions and villainous retainers embedded deeply like weeds in the palace." As it points to the deposed Queen YUN and JANG Nok-su as the causes of the king's tyranny, the film mends a wounded patriarchal order once again by restoring the king to the position of family head.[16] The scapegoating of women here may have been a "masculine perspective," and it may also have been intended simply to sustain dramatic tension through a clear relationship of confrontation among major characters. Or it could be both. While it may be said that Yeonsan's pathological obsession and lust for revenge were historical facts, the fact that other political factors were eliminated or treated as trivial in the film provides a glimpse into SHIN Sang-ok's view of history. Thus, the director may have had the view that, even though politics and power are not ugly things in themselves, an individual can at least be destroyed if he enters the heart of it or comes up close. This kind of attitude, which does not view historical facts in terms of the power structure or social conflicts, is likely related in some way to the director's own

15. BAEK Mun-im, "Historical Pieces and Horror Films: The Case of Shin Sang-ok," *Minjok Munhaksa Yeongu (Studies of Ethnic Cultural History)*, Vol. 20, June 2002, pp. 316-317. Take from PARK A-na, "A Study of Shin Sang-ok's Film Production and Genres (Melodramas and Historical Pieces) from 1952 to 1975)," Chung-Ang University, 2003, p. 51.
16. PARK A-na, same as above, p. 52.

Prince Yeonsan, 1961

personal experience. An impressionable twenty-year-old youth when Korea was liberated from Japan, he was witness to people's sympathies for and against Japan and to their changes in ideology. Following liberation, he saw bloody confrontations between left and right, war and its devastation, the collapse of the RHEE Syngman administration and the military coup d'état of PARK Chung-hee. Such historical experiences likely contributed to his privatization of history and to the formation of an individualistic and nihilistic view of history.

"My thoughts on film have also changed a great deal. I also learned a lot from the analysis of Korean history that I heard from the noted historian LEE Na-yeong, with whom I shared a prison cell. To someone like me, who had always used the fact that I was busy as an excuse never to take time for self-examination, that time was an unexpected opportunity to replenish myself fully. Making films in North Korea, I thought a lot about the social functions of film."[17] These words

17. Ibid., p. 121.

summarize the thoughts that occurred within SHIN as he spent time in a North Korean prison. He would subsequently direct *The Secret Envoy Who Never Returned* (1984) in North Korea. Of course the film emerged from a compromise with the North Korean government, but it shows traces of breaking away from an individualist perspective. Following his escape from North Korea, he would make *Mayumi* (1990) and *Vanished* (1994), political and historical works that dealt respectively with the explosion of a KAL airliner and the story surrounding the death of KIM Hyung-wook, head of the Korean Central Intelligence Agency. Here he was critical of both the North and South Korean administrations; he had any traces of the historical privatization that he had shown in films like *Prince Yeonsan* and tackled universal issues of good and evil and problems of political power head on. In most of his films dealing with historical incidents, he had given individual interpretations or historical adaptations for dramatic interest. Had he changed after his studies in prison? SHIN wrote, "I hated the left, which took foolish risks, and I hated the right, which had no morals. It is the essence of an artist that he must always resist everything that suppresses the human, so it is inevitable that the two will clash."[18] Perhaps SHIN had been performing numerous experiments for 50 years in order to turn these words into film.

Fourth, there are films that deal with customs and are set in past eras. These include *The Red Gate* (1962), in which a widow who is forced to live in chastity following her husband's death has a carnal affair with a farm hand and runs away; *Women of the Joseon Dynasty* (1969), which tells of a woman who has a child against palace rules and flees; and *A Thousand Year Old Fox* (1969), a horror film set in the Silla Era in which a general's wife, killed because of the queen's jealousy, is reborn in the body of a 1000-year-old fox and participates in a love triangle. SHIN explained: "Even if I want to make a film with a social message, it's impossible, so I use the form of the historical drama and express it indirectly. Examples of this are films like *The Red Gate* and *Women of the Joseon Dynasty* [...] I saw the structure of repression as essential the same thing as the system of

18. Ibid., p. 144.

political and social repression that strangles us today [...] On the surface, it may appear to be the "image of the vengeful woman dominated by fate," but if you view it in a little more depth, you can grasp a stronger will to resist internally rather than external rebellion."[19]

The Red Gate, 1962

Among SHIN's historical dramas, there are almost no examples of cases like the Japanese *chûshinkura* dramas or the Korean "General YI Sun-sin film" that functioned as ideological tools to mobilize the nation for the sake of a certain administration. The only one would be *LEE Seung-man and the Independence Movement*. But he said of the making of *The Sino-Japanese War and the Heroic Queen Min* that it was actually "planned at a time when the whole nation was making a lot of noise about the Korea-Japan summit, with the idea that we should properly educate the citizenry, and especially the young people, about our modern history. We finished it in three months so that it could be released before the summit was realized."[20] However, it would be difficult to apply the example of *The Sino-Japanese War and the Heroic Queen Min* unchanged to other films. SHIN's historical view or method of reading appears to have been a method of reconstructing or evaluating through personal historical imagination in order to resist a system in which the interpretation of most history was determined by the

19. Ibid., p. 88.
20. Ibid., p. 90.

official analysis of the ruling class of the time. If one accepts this claim, it is possible to take many of his historical pieces as works intended to arouse caution toward the Japanese empire (e.g., *The Three-Day Reign*) or as films made as proxies to symbolize the oppressive structures of the times (e.g., *The Red Gate*). But most of his historical pieces, including his most famous work *Prince Yeonsan*, can only be judged as the privatized reading of history, adopting historical facts merely as subject matter and focused on ratcheting up dramatic tension while flavoring them with personal imagination.

Melodrama

The melodramas of SHIN Sang-ok began with his 1952 debut, *The Evil Night*, and would diverge in 1958 into films with two entirely different faces: *A Flower in Hell* and *A College Woman's Confession*. If *A Flower in Hell* carried on the tone of *The Evil Night* in its portrayal of the gloomy postwar city, *A College Woman's Confession* depicts a woman overcoming that gloom. If the former showed the "anxiety of modernity," the latter essentially showed the "promise of modernity." Before being a melodrama, *A Flower in Hell* is film showing traces of the influences that early Korean film received from the outside. The rough Yeong-sik is the kept man of Sonya, a *yangbuin*, and one day their relationship becomes a triangle when his younger brother Dong-sik comes to Seoul. Sonya mimics the pinup girls of Hollywood films in her appearance and behavior, and this culminates in a scene where she seduces Dong-sik in a swimsuit on the banks of the Han River. Another lengthy scene shows her dancing at a party for an American army unit and is reminiscent of a scene from a musical. Yeong-sik and his cohorts take advantage of the party to rob the PX warehouse, and Sonya, blinded by love, reports him. What follows is a gangster film fugitive story of chasing and being chased. Sonya and Yeong-sik end up rolling around in the mud fighting, and the femme fatale ends up dying at Yeong-sik's hands. Like this, *A Flower in Hell* contains a jumble of elements from various Hollywood genres: melodrama, film noir, musical, gangster film. Sonya represents a new image of the woman, revealing an uneasy modern look. She dares to covet the younger brother of her husband, she reports her husband's crime in order to realize her love, and she actively adopts a Western appearance. The film shows uncertain aspects of modernity by faithfully revealing its materialism, egoism and snobbery. Meanwhile, Dong-sik arrives in Seoul an innocent, shocked and dismayed by the image of modernity, and decides to return home to the country, where the purity of the pre-modern remains. At this point, Sonya is wandering, between the self-interest of the modern and the purity of the pre-modern. *A Flower in Hell* follows in the footsteps of *The Evil Night* by faithfully representing the dismal postwar mood. It appears to have shared with that film a gloomy sense about "what follows the escape from poverty."

A College Woman's Confession was inspired by a French film called *Betrayal*, and in fact there was also a Japanese film called *A Female Lawyer's Confession*. The film tells of a poor woman moving up in the world. She has been hurt many times by men. When she gets behind in her rent, the owner of the dormitory comes on to her, and when she goes to interview for a job the boss makes sexual demands. She pretends to be the lost daughter of an Assemblyman and is accepted into his home as a treasured daughter, eventually becoming a lawyer. As a lawyer, she defends an unwed mother who is suspected of killing the man who betrayed her, sternly reproaching social inequality and men's pre-modern view of the sexes. But the wife of the Assemblyman learns that she is not his real daughter. A brief conflict follows, but in the end the

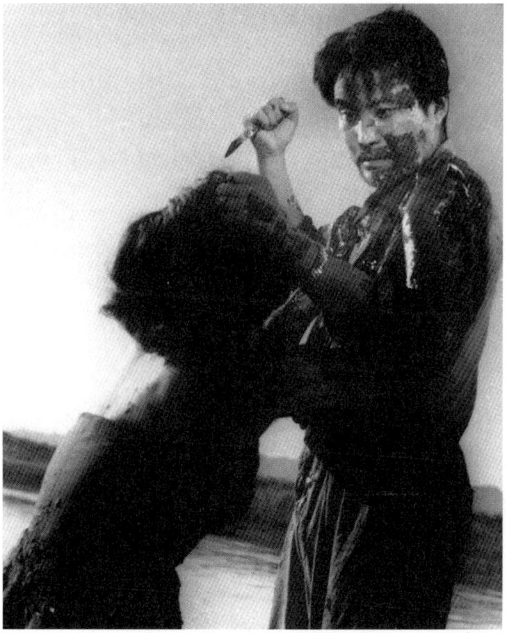

A Flower in Hell, 1958

wife understands the young woman's past and decides to keep everything secret. The main character in this film is a righteous woman who has succeeded in society and uses the power of her success for other disadvantaged women. This character is something even from a present-day standpoint, so it is not difficult to imagine the envious gazes she would have gotten in 1958.[21] Also, there is solidarity between female characters. The three women—the single mother/killer, the heroine and the mother—understand and comfort each other over the things that they have had to endure merely because they are women, and their tight bond pulls the drama along. SHIN's attempt to raise women's social consciousness and show female solidarity as a model clearly would have held meaning in terms of social education. However, the plot has a structure that would lose decisive strength if the heroine did not enter the upper reaches of society through deception. The film was a major hit at the box office as well, and its star CHOI Eun-hee, who became an instant star with this film, may have seemed like some unapproachable modern mirage. So CHOI may have been a heroine who made women viewers feel both catharsis within the theater and frustration outside of it. If one views the course of SHIN's melodramas in this sense, he clearly speaks of "what follows the escape from poverty" through this film, namely that "happiness after the escape from poverty" is only possible through the safety of the patriarchal system and efforts to enter the upper class. Women unable to do so must remain patient. This point is clearly revealed in his next melodrama.

The "college woman" presented as a model image of the woman, like the heroines in *Evergreen Tree* and *Rice*, was nowhere to be seen in the four melodramas SHIN would go on to make in 1959. In *A Sister's Garden* (1959), in which an older daughter and younger daughter play a seesaw game of love over three men (one man whom their father told one daughter to marry on his deathbed, one man who helped their father economically and one middle-aged man whose disease was cured by their father's medical methods), women are not active entities. When the father who protected them dies, the two daughters await the

21. In 2008 as well, a drama called *Seven Female Lawyers* is being shown in Japan to great popularity.

A College Woman's Confession, 1958

love of other men, or else it appears that their destiny is decided by the men's decisions. One of the things that function as an important variable in this fatal decision is "money." Amid an uncertain financial situation, the women must wait for the decision of men one way or another. *Dongsimcho*, which tells the story of the love between a war widow and a publishing company director who is engaged to his boss's daughter, ends with the woman, a mother with a fully grown daughter for whom remarrying is unsuited to the conventions of the times, leaving Seoul. Here too the love begins with the publishing company executive helping the war widow, who owns a dressmaking shop but is harried by debts. What SHIN showed in these two melodramas was the image of women without economic power who had to be protected in the name of love. The melodrama *To the Last Day*, released the following year in 1960, tells the story of a wife whose husband is paralyzed from the waist down due to a war wound. She briefly shares an impulsive romance with a young man before establishing a community for war widows and creating a new future with them. Poverty is still something of the present, and a full comeback from the war has not been reached.

Another group of melodramas followed, including *SEONG Chun-hyang* (1961), *My Mother and Her Guest* (1961) and *Deaf Samryong-i* (1964). *SEONG Chun-hyang* was based on a Korean traditional tale with more than 100 versions that has also been produced several times in film and television drama form. LEE, a son of a high-ranking aristocratic family, shares a passionate romance with Chun-hyang, whose mother is a former *gisaeng* (a type of Korean female entertainer), but when his father is ordered to Seoul, the two are forced to say goodbye. At this point, the region's newly appointed magistrate, BYEON, tries to force Chun-hyang into becoming his mistress, but she refuses him. This refusal places Chun-hyang in danger of losing her life. Meanwhile, LEE passes the *gwageo* state examination and becomes a secret royal commissioner, punishing BYEON for plundering the citizens and rescuing Chun-hyang so that they can love again. Viewed from modern standards, Chun-hyang's attitude seems proper, but when one considers the time at which the film is set, it seems reckless. Because of the difference in their social status, their love was never going to be realized easily; there was no guarantee that LEE would not change his mind after leaving for Seoul; LEE was a profligate whose chances of passing the examination were rather low; and even if he did pass, it would not have been easy for him to work to find her. The essential point of contention here is class difference rather than the man's fidelity. The story of Chun-hyang is beloved by many for showing a love that transcends such class differences, but the love that overcomes that barrier is really only possible because of Chun-hyang's reckless bravery. Praise for her imprudent

To the Last Day, 1960

behavior that puts her life at risk is also praise for a femininity that has faith in an uncertain love. *Deaf Samryong-i* tells the story of a deaf servant who feels a chaste and devoted love for the new mistress who is abused by his master. Here too the framework consists of praise for the deaf servant's life-threatening love, a love that can never be realized. *My Mother and Her Guest* begins with a woman, widowed at a young age with a young daughter, who brings her older brother's friend into her house as a boarder. Without any events bringing them together directly, the two of them fall in love through a kind of telepathy. The young man finally cannot take it and writes a letter to her, but their love is not realized. While spiritual love is emphasized, the taboo against a widow remarrying is also emphasized as something beautiful(?). What the three films share is that they are all dramas based on preexisting works, with a sense of stability in that their narratives are solid and the story is not advanced through random events or motivations. Also, dialogue, expressions and emotions are manipulated expertly based on this stability of narrative, and the images are exceedingly warm and sentimental as well. In particular, *My Mother and Her Guest* is enriched by the winsome role of the young daughter and the love between the maid and the egg salesman, which seems to substitute for the love of the boarder and the mother. The reckless love of *SEONG Chun-hyang*, the forbidden love in *My Mother and Her Guest* and the devoted love in *Deaf Samryong-i* are all created by the limitations and taboos of the times, but SHIN Sang-ok basically expresses them as values that must be observed. The question of which is more beneficial or worthwhile—criticizing and calling into question the limitations and taboos of the times or praising the beautiful humanity that flowers within them—is left to the judgment of each viewer.

SEONG Chun-hyang, 1961

Finally, I would like to make reference to *Romance Papa*, (1960), a comedy that holds an unusual position among SHIN's films. A father who works at an insurance company and is called

"Romance Papa" by his children lives harmoniously with his wife and five children. The oldest daughter graduates from university and marries a man who works at a meteorological observatory, while the oldest son fools his parents into thinking that he is attending university and works at a film set in order to become a director. The second daughter is a college student, while the second son and the youngest daughter are high school students. It is difficult to support such a large family on the father's salary, but he is an optimist who shelters his family with laughter. However, a wave of staff cuts hits the insurance company, and the father, a devoted employee, is laid off because of his age. Worried that his family will feel discouraged, he does not tell them that he has lost his job. The son and daughters find out, but pretend not to know and look for a way to comfort their father. On his birthday, the whole family gathers to share a happy time together. Filled with humor, the film clearly shows the time's image of a petit bourgeois household, as well as the generation gap and the powerless patriarch. In addition, there is *Romance Gray* (1963), which tells the farcical love story of an adulterous boss. These films clearly reveal the image of working life at the time, as well as depictions of sexual mores and the conflict between the modern and the pre-modern. When we view these films by SHIN, we may think that the world now may be a bit tough but is still a livable place, or that the family is the only remaining refuge for protecting people in a rapidly changing world.

At the same time, these films share similar tendencies with Japanese films made in the 1950s under the names of the "salaryman series" and the "company boss series."[22] They can be seen as a phenomenon based in

Romance Papa, 1960

22. GU Gyeon-seo, *Japanese Film and Temporality*, J&C, 2006, p. 329. These works include salaryman films such as *Santô Juyaku (Third Class Executives)* (1957) and films comically depicting the adultery of bosses such as *Shachô Sandaiki* (1958).

a homogeneity of the times that necessarily accompanied rapid postwar modernization and sought to portray the lives of the lower middle class.

I have attempted to encapsulate this discussion of SHIN Sang-ok, the man who was called the emperor of Korean film in the 1960s, with the concepts of "the escape from poverty," "privatized history" and "melodrama." Like most Korean directors, SHIN lost considerable force in the late 1960s in terms of the discovery of thriving subject matter and expression that he had shown before as a result of severe censorship. But even in that situation, there are works such as *Eunuch* and *A Thousand Year Old Fox*, which were not dealt with in earnest in this essay but which sufficiently lend themselves to treatment as allegories of a different kind. In particular, 1964's *Red Muffler* was a box office success for that era. I would like to add that it contained male friendships and relationships with the women around them that were a subject worthy of close examination, and that several scenes in which SHIN attempted to break through technical limitations of the time would long remain notable achievements in Korean film history. There are also the films that SHIN made while in North Korea, but I have eliminated them from mention in this discussion of SHIN's works because I did not deem it appropriate.

If someone were to ask me what SHIN Sang-ok pursued to the last through his films or what he considered most important among the endeavors of film, I would say "entertainment." To SHIN, "entertainment" was not something that brought personal honors or fame and fortune, but something like a destiny not only for the grand enterprise of Shin Films, which he ran, but for all of Korean cinema. It was a choice he made for himself. Yet his major works lose nothing in comparison with those of other remarkable Korean directors. When I used the expression here of "the escape from poverty," it was because I had in mind the surmounting of a pressing modern psychological state or a transitional social environment which cannot be encompassed merely through the lately overused word "modernity." No matter what cultural interpretation or lofty rhetoric I may use, there is likely no more precise word one can use to describe Korean society directly after the war in the 1950s than "poverty." This is because any signs of moving forward to a new world might have been given from outside or the hope of a small few. Even in this state, *A Flower in Hell* succeeded surprisingly in mixing Hollywood genres, and it is that valuable for it. Also, I hope that the words "privatized history" will not be taken simply in a negative vein. The adoption of a leftist stance or the insertion of communitarianism in film (which of course would not have been easy with the censorship situation of the times) is not just something that would have been difficult. SHIN Sang-ok simply interpreted the incidents and characters of history with his own view. This aspect of SHIN Sang-ok is also "another history." What can be verified in his various historical dramas and period pieces is that SHIN Sang-ok was "an absolute liberal who considered things in terms of entertainment." Of course, I also find it just to criticize this aspect from another perspective.

Finally, the "eye" that SHIN Sang-ok showed in his work in melodrama, which could be called the best genre in terms of showing the contemporary world, was something difficult to grasp. South Korean society in the 1960s was at a time where a modern sense of society had just been set in motion by the military dictatorship following the chaos of liberation in 1945 and the war from 1950 to 1953. Let us consider for a moment the confusion in values that occurred together with the social confusion of the time. Conflict and confusion existed in almost all areas: confrontations between left and right, gender issues, furthering and disintegration of the patriarchal system, Western culture and native culture, modern values and pre-modern values, the values of the military administration that succeeded the Japanese militarist culture and the values of democracy. SHIN seems to have made films at times from the standards of modern values, at times from the standards of democratic values, and at times from the standards of patriarchal values. The image conveyed is a confusing one, but I think that the value he most esteemed may have been a patriarchal and somewhat pre-modern one. However, he may have felt that the standards of his own values were perpetual values inherent in all humans. This too can be considered "another history."

SHIN Sang-ok and the SHIN Sang-ok System

This essay was written in a somewhat personal manner in order to tell several stories related to the great Korean director SHIN Sang-ok. While discussing his Shin Films, the first and last major Korean system, I would like to speak of SHIN Sang-ok for whom the impression of a master of film art remains more strongly than that of someone who was effectively a CEO. In order to do so, I feel that an explanation about the author is in order. Up until now, I have viewed SHIN Sang-ok as one of the figures who ruined Korean film. He was someone who would do anything for film, even joining up with the military dictatorship during the PARK Chung-hee administration, and I thought that his influence on Korean film was negative. As an example of this, one could first cite the making of *LEE Seung-man and the Independence Movement*. LEE Seung-man (also written as RHEE Syngman) was a figure driven out of the office of President through the protests of

Korean citizens. SHIN had made the film that was essentially propaganda intended to continue LEE's control of the government, so viewing it this way was natural. I even viewed *Evergreen Tree* and *Rice*, subsequent works considered among his most important, as films conforming to the PARK Chung-hee government's policy of modernization. There are many ways to overcome the situation of a poor economy, but PARK chose only the methods of dictatorial politics and nurturing a small number of conglomerate groups. As a result, many people were unjustly executed or imprisoned for political crimes under the terrible policies of the dictatorship, and the workers suffering through low-income hard labor endured miserable lives. It was natural to criticize SHIN Sang-ok, who had supported this administration through his films. In another book in this series, *JANG Sun-woo*, the author Tony Rayns introduced one of my essays by calling me a "leftist critic"; I don't know what basis he had for using that expression, but I think that my stubborn stance on SHIN Sang-ok may have had some influence. However, it would be natural to view my position not as a leftist opinion but as a general democratic attitude. I think there are perhaps too few people with this kind of general democratic attitude among the film scholars and critics in South Korea. I also think that if Tony Rayns lived in South Korea with a democratic attitude, he might feel the same way as I do.

I have never written anything concentrating on SHIN Sang-ok. I may have mentioned him in some other essays with a different character. Even now, I hold a critical view toward the director CHOI In-kyu, who SHIN Sang-ok himself declared to be one of his mentors in film and for whom SHIN did the work of assistant director. He did pro-Japanese national policy films during the Japanese occupation, and then, once Korea was liberated, he enjoyed a big success with *Hurrah! For Freedom*, a film that told the story of armed independence fighters resisting the Japanese. The attitude of "If I can make films, I can do anything" passed from CHOI In-kyu to SHIN Sang-ok, and from SHIN to LEE Chang-ho (an up-and-coming Korean director who would become a major figure in the 1980s), and I think that it became an indirect cause of moral indifference in all of Korean film, or at least an axis in the formation of such a climate. Furthermore, though it is difficult to verify, Korean filmmaking laws were for the most part established or amended at the time when SHIN Sang-ok was working most actively, functioning as a toxic element inhibiting the development of Korean film for decades. It was also the opinion of the entire Korean film world that SHIN Sang-ok was the biggest villain in terms of this era's bad film laws. (In his autobiography and interviews, SHIN not only strenuously denies this, he also provides an explanation for the reason why this view was accepted.) In addition, questions remain about his activity in North Korea and kidnapping or possibly voluntary journey to the North, which is difficult to verify outside of the director's own claims. To sum it up, I did not have a negative view of SHIN Sang-ok because I myself had the perspective of a leftist critic or because I deny that he has a few outstanding works. It was because he had made films supporting the dictatorship, and because he had played a clear role in the creation of negative currents in Korean film. To this were added profound doubts about his role in the enactment of bad film laws.

But my verdict began to go through changes after I met the man directly. In 2004, he visited me while I was serving as director of the Korean Film Archive. Looking just the same as in the pictures I had seen of him, he smiled and spoke in a soft voice. He had come because he was about to donate a few of the films that he had made in North Korea, and he wanted to ask for technical treatment, copies of the prints and special storage. Naturally, his request was accepted. He was no longer the legendary figure running the vast enterprise of Shin Films or trudging into river water with a camera on his shoulder wearing suit pants and dress shoes. He was a thoughtful individual, humble about life and fate, who was facing death and wanted to put some things in order. After that, I began to think that I might have had some misunderstanding. I went on to watch every one of the Korean films from the 1960s available at the Korean Film Archive, and I came to have a different judgment about his films. Now, four years later, I have watched his films once again and organized data he left behind in interviews and articles in order to write this book about him. Some mixed feelings arose about whether my judgment was totally correct, and I also had the thought that an understanding of him of a different kind was necessary. Of course, this judgment was not made because I had changed my political perspective or because I am a Buddhist.

Mentors

SHIN Sang-ok had three cinematic mentors. In his autobiography *I, Was Film* (Random House Korea, 2007), in a section entitled "NA Woon-gyu, My Spiritual Mentor," SHIN wrote the following: "When you view his films today, they may seem very rough or immature. But in them, you can sense an intense spirit that seems like it will tear through the screen and leap out at you, and that spirit blazed up into an intense flame through an interaction with the viewer [...] Around that time, the level of Korean cinema was at a point where people cheered just seeing a person moving on the screen, but NA Woon-gyu struggled in his films to portray people who were suffering and inspire a national spirit that was disappearing [...] I think of NA Woon-gyu as both the first cinematic creator in Korean film and almost the only one even today [...] Of the 20 films NA left behind, at least 15 of them are films that he wrote, directed and starred in himself. When you consider his short life and the production environment of the time, he was really an almost mythical figure who gave everything for film."[1] NA Woon-gyu was essentially SHIN Sang-ok's first cinematic mentor. (None of NA's films remain extant today.)

His second mentor was CHOI In-kyu, director of *Hurrah! For Freedom*. SHIN wrote: "I learned the foundations of film, and the technical aspects in particular, from CHOI In-kyu. It was also then that I really systematized into one all of the fragmentary knowledge that I had obtained through the countless films I had seen since I was a child. Because I had seen so many films and been so deeply into film, I think my education was that fast. What I learned at that time became a firm support for my cinematic career. CHOI In-kyu was basically my second mentor. If I learned the foundations of film and the creator's spirit through the works left

1. SHIN Sang-ok, *I, Was Film*, Random House Korea, 2007, p. 28.

behind by NA Woon-gyu, I learned all of the core techniques of real film production from CHOI In-kyu."[2] In the same book, SHIN provided an introduction to the capabilities and obstinacy as an individual of CHOI In-kyu the technical pioneer. He recounts how CHOI borrowed a country house when shooting a film. It was impossible to shoot the whole house because of a persimmon tree in the yard, so CHOI waited until the owner left the house, chopped the tree down, and continued with the filming. SHIN also mentioned somewhere about how he thought he inherited from CHOI In-kyu the idea that he could do anything for film, and he recalled that it was also CHOI's influence that led him to shoot and edit his films himself and to boldly, even recklessly, invest in the introduction of new equipment and technology.[3] But in another interview, he talked about how there were other factors as well, namely that the wartime situation made it so that he had no choice but to do most of the process himself and that, because his own camera technique was better, he had no need to hire a cameraman and waste time debating and compromising on everything with him. Also, he said that developing was done in Japan until the early 1960s, so if anything came out wrong, he would have to go to Japan again, so he had no choice but to do it himself.[4] In another interview, while acknowledging CHOI In-kyu's excellent points, SHIN added another frank assessment: "But CHOI, while outstanding in technical areas, is not a thinker. And that guy, if you give him a good script you get a good film, and if you give him a bad script, the film doesn't come out right. He also doesn't really know the character of his films. He was a really pitiable guy."[5] SHIN regarded Charlie Chaplin as his final mentor. Of course, he grew up watching films by many foreign directors, but in the following interview one can sense a special quality when it comes to Chaplin. SHIN says, "The reason I like Chaplin the best is—and this is in his autobiography as well—he said, I was busy earning money for myself, and other people called it art. He said

2. Ibid., pp. 34-35.
3. Ibid., p. 42.
4. Interview with AHN Tae-geun, which was conducted on November 16, 2001.
5. CHOE In-ho, "Shin Sang-ok's Films, Shin Sang-ok's Art," *Monthly Joseon*, October 1983, p. 272. This interview appears to have been recorded 4 or 5 years before, around 1978, before SHIN went to North Korea.

that he wanted a social quality to it, but at the same time enjoyment. He put entertainment into it [...] After that, there's a scene with a demonstration, and the demonstrators are these laborers protesting and waging a labor movement. He's holding a flag and trying to get out of the street, and at some point he's standing in front and he's become like a conductor. It becomes like the truth, like he's going ahead as the leader. This is a very sharp criticism of modern society and civilization, but he made it so that the people watching laugh and enjoy everything. I think that's the ideal kind of film. I think he really hit the nail on the head when he said that he worked hard making films to earn money and it became art when they said it was art."[6]

One could say that SHIN learned the spirit of the director from NA Woon-gyu, the importance of technique from CHOI In-kyu, and the innate destiny of film to inevitably compromise with the viewer and the spirit of not losing oneself within that destiny from Charlie Chaplin. It certainly seems that he could be called a disciple of NA, CHOI and Chaplin in that he made films with his whole body, he carried the camera himself, and he considered audience tastes first before creative color and artistic evaluation. But maybe only SHIN himself could know how faithful a disciple he was.

Shin Films and Bad Film Laws

Shin Films, the studio operated by SHIN Sang-ok, could be fairly called one half of the Korean film world. It was so when he had a studio in Yongsan, and it was more so after he took over the film studio in Anyang.

After an early success with *A College Woman's Confession* (1958), he racked up big hits with films like *SEONG Chun-hyang* (1961) and *Prince Yeonsan* (1961), allowing Shin Films to assume a place as the biggest major studio in Korea and attract countless house directors and actors, at one point reaching a peak of

6. Interview with AHN Tae-geun mentioned above.

250 employees. While Shin Films was Korea's biggest and best film studio, it was also a school for figures in Korean film. There was even a shuttle bus for staff members, and the studio boasted the means to have a daily newspaper in which line-up advertisements were regularly printed for the films being produced or released at the time. But this kind of large-scale investment and management gave rise to economic difficulties that continued from the mid-1960s. Following the absorption of the Anyang lot in 1967, the studio was even further in the red, and there would be the constant threat of bankruptcy. Even SHIN's wife, CHOI Eun-hee, a house performer at the studio, was driven into a situation where she had to earn money by appearing in other films. However, in the process, it seems that SHIN was a figure envied and resented by many.

In a conversation with CHOE In-ho, the topic of children came up, and SHIN said something completely off the wall: "I've never once looked at a child and thought it was cute. I often heard myself called 'cold-blooded' when it came to work because in the old days I was a loner, and I think they may have been right."[7] This attitude may have been the cause of SHIN's making many enemies for himself. In addition, he treated newspaper reporters with a dismissive attitude, and this may have been one reason for artistic judgments of his films always falling short. LEE Myeong-won, a film critic and former newspaper reporter, scoffed in a criticism of many other aspects of SHIN, "You could call him a realist who ruthlessly eliminated anything that could be the slightest bit of a minus in the business of film. He behaved like a realist in the way that he sought to expand the plus column so much that he became cozy with the powers that be in the political world."[8] SHIN's complacent attitude, seemingly dismissive treatment of the media, and enterprising, forward-moving approach may have fanned negative opinions such as the criticism by LEE Myeong-won quoted here. He would even say the following: "Even if we were able to solve a minimum of mechanical issues, I don't think we had an academic background in film [...] If I may exaggerate a little, I think that YU Hyun-mok, KIM Ki-young and I have all had pretty good lives as

7. CHOE In-ho, same 1983, p. 265.
8. LEE Myeong-won, "Shin Sang-ok, Film's Soldier of Fortune," *Sedae (Generation)*, March 1967, p. 288.

It's Not Her Sin, 1959

directors and it would be OK for us to take a step back. Let's just say that what we did wasn't anything." These words are reflective, but at the same time cannot help betraying an exceedingly arrogant attitude.

The person really in charge of managing Shin Films until the mid-1960s was HWANG Nam, a former actor. During the war, he met and joined up with SHIN, appearing in *The Evil Night* and running the Seoul Film Company together with him. They were passionate youths who decided to try making films with a group system. HWANG was Korean film's first planner and highlighted the role of the planner in film. He also planned *A College Woman's Confession* and *It's Not Her Sin*, which would provide major funding to begin Shin Films. He parted ways with SHIN around the time of *Red Muffler* (1964), though it is not clear whether he left because of Shin Films' poor financial situation or the situation deteriorated after HWANG's departure. Perhaps both were factors.

HWANG remarked cynically about SHIN: "I came to Seoul with SHIN Sang-ok and made movies, and we started with the name of Seoul Pictures. SHIN was the director and I did the planning [...] SHIN is a director, but he followed my directions when doing films and theater. When we first started out it was a mess."[9] He also said, "So he had no choice but to serve as director for the Hollywood Theater. But after SHIN paid back some of the debts, his ideas changed again. He's a greedy person. I went out to the country briefly, and when I came back he had sold off the Hollywood Theater."[10]

Such criticism and jealousy of SHIN Sang-ok was likely recognized more broadly in connection with policy management in Korean film at the time and contributed toward solidifying the awareness of people in film. SHIN claimed that he shared no responsibility in the enactment of what came to be called Korean's bad film laws. But it appears that people did not share that opinion.

In his interview with LEE Gi-rim, SHIN said the following: "At that time, there were maybe 100 or so film companies, something like that? Everybody said "I can

9. Korean Film Archive, "Speaking About Korean Film: The Korean Cinema of the 1950s," LEE Chae, 2004, p. 415.
10. Ibid., p. 420.

make a film" and all went out to make movies. There were a lot of unsavory incidents that occurred as side effects from the "independent" movement. Because film is gambling, people ran off without making the film, things like that, or if the film went bust they would disappear. The military government, they were the ones who thought, "That won't do, we have to fix it." And so they reorganized the film companies. But you have to view it as a myopic policy. I talked about this before, but just because you have facilities, it doesn't mean you can make films.

"After their reorganization, there were maybe 16 or so film companies, and the contradictory part was that there were so many side effects, since they didn't do the research all at once. You had equipment going here and there, and all you had to do was rent a warehouse and you had a 200 *pyeong* (approximately 660 square meter) studio. The 200-*pyeong* standard was so vague that it was enough just to have 200 *pyeong*, with no standards, regardless of whether it was soundproofed or if you could even shoot there. It was total trial and error.[11]

"Some people think that because I had a big film studio I made laws so that people without them couldn't make films and that I suppressed them, but that's not true at all. Film laws were entirely the idea of the soldiers. At first, I stayed away from the laws. I did become close to PARK Chung-hee because of *Evergreen Tree*. He said that he cried after watching it. After that was the start of the Evergeen movement and the Saemaeul movements, and because of that we grew closer, and then there was the selloff of the Anyang lot. That's how you can look at it."[12]

This is how SHIN defended himself. But at the time, it seems to have been public opinion or rumor that SHIN had contributed in a major way to the formation of bad film laws. LEE Myeong-won writes: "SHIN Sang-ok has been thought to be the only major figure representing Korean cinema. He has many flaws. But if you take him away, there's no one left. This was taken as kind of a given both within the film world and even outside of it. It wouldn't have just been

11. LEE Gi-rim, "Korean Film Memoirs, Shin Sang-ok 14," *Cine 21*, 2003
12. LEE Gi-rim, "Korean Film Memoirs, Shin Sang-ok 12," *Cine 21*, 2003

because of this, but during that time he had been appointed head of the Korean Film Workers Association three times, and had real influence on the direction of the relevant authorities' film policy."[13] LEE goes on to claim that SHIN stepped down as a representative for film producers in order to run for a nationwide Assembly seat and eyed the position of chairman for the directors' committee of the Motion Pictures Association of Korea.[14] However, this too does not jibe with SHIN's claims.

As seen here, claims about SHIN's contribution to the formation of bad laws in the Korean film world are divergent. But in any case, he did meet with the President around once a month at the time and become close with the Prime Minister KIM Jong-pil, and it that sense cannot be free from such criticisms, regardless of the truth or falsehood of such claims.

Despair in South Korea, Abduction to North Korea

In 1975, Shin Films' registration was revoked because of the insertion of a few seconds of film that did not pass the censors into the trailer for *The Rose and the Wild Dog*, and after borrowing the name of another company to make a few films, SHIN went to Hong Kong in search of CHOI Eun-hee, who had gone missing. SHIN too would end up in North Korea. At the time, the two were divorced. The revocation of SHIN's film company license over a trifling issue came at a time when the PARK Chung-hee administration was putting forth absurd policies in order to move into a dictatorship, but it seems that SHIN's sensitive reaction to the film's censorship was the major contributing factor. According to SHIN, the atmosphere of hostility was forming against him, as matters such as his resistance to the government's film policy and censorship system, the scandal involving OH Mi-su and his divorce from CHOI Eun-hee came one after another. On censorship,

13. LEE Myeong-won, 1967, p. 282.
14. Ibid., p. 283.

SHIN said sarcastically that how much officials in charge of film censorship at the Minister of Culture and Information would cut with films was determined by whether they had a good breakfast on that day or not. When the novelist CHOE In-ho, who once had directed a film himself, mentioned his own experience with censorship officials, SHIN Sang-ok said, "Well, it's OK if they cut however much they want at the Minister of Culture and Information. My only wish, though, is that they would just leave me alone to film."[15] Together with this kind of awareness, it is not difficult to imagine how unpleasant and even detestable the open criticism of censorship SHIN leveled after becoming chairman of the Korea Film Directors' Society must have been to PARK Chung-hee, who thought he had helped SHIN.[16]

It is the official interpretation that he was kidnapped to North Korea by the North Korean government, but it is also true that many people in Korean cinema assume that he went there on his own. His situation at the time, in his words, was that he "ran all around for three years requesting that the permit for Shin Films be reinstated, but there was nowhere to turn. Those three years when I was forcibly kept away from film represented the most difficult, frustrating and unbearable period of my life."[17] In addition, he also despaired of the reality of Korean film. To him, Korean film was despair itself: severe censorship, the inability for actors to even have costumes suited to their roles, the unavoidably low standards of obligatory Korean films made to meet a quota for foreign importation, the ridiculously low production standards in comparison with Japan's high production standards, and the lack of technology and impossibly low standards in areas such as film art and music. It is easy to imagine his despair: If he had still been running Shin Films, he could at least have found a starting point for improvements in those areas, but with his film company having been forced out of business, it is easy to imagine his despair. All the more so for the man who said, "My dream is the

15. CHOE In-ho, same interview as above. pp. 267, 277. SHIN Sang-ok criticizes censorship twice in the interview, as well as the Korean film laws and the landscape of Korean film.
16. SHIN Sang-ok, 2007, p. 114.
17. Ibid., p. 114.

'commercialization and industrialization of film.' In order for Korean cinema to make a leap forward, I think that a Korean-style major system needs to take root and stable film capital needs to be formed."[18]

At the same time, he also said the following about his psychological state just before his 1978 abduction: "Now that I'm older and wiser, I don't like strange films, and if you want to make good films, it's difficult to do at the rate of one a year. You have to get an idea and write a good script, and if you want it to be appropriate for the world market, since you can't just show it in Daegu and Seoul, that costs money, and it has to be accepted in that market, so those kinds of problems emerge [...] Lately I've been thinking. Why are films made in a totalitarian state able to win awards at the Cannes Film Festival? We have fewer constraints, so why can't we make such films? This is a pretty important question [...] when the constraints are really severe, once production is started, you don't think about money, you just focus all of your efforts. So you can be evaluated on that. But we have neither."[19] Officially, SHIN was kidnapped by force and made films while receiving hospitable treatment in the North before his dramatic escape. However, we can catch a glimpse of how SHIN Sang-ok had already developed enough of an issue awareness to make films in a totalitarian (socialist) society. Of course, he had already had the experience of coming South due to the ideological conflicts in the North and losing both parents in the war. He was too individualistic to be a socialist ideologically, and he was liberal, but at the same time believed in the Korean-style Confucian values. Thus, it is difficult to imagine that he chose to go North of his own volition. But that judgment comes into question when one considers his situation at the time, or how he shared similar thinking and actions with his mentor CHOI In-kyu, who was willing to do anything for film.[20]

18. Ibid., p. 18.
19. CHOE In-ho, same interview as above, p. 271.
20. Interview with AHN Tae-geun. In an attached interview with YU Hyun-mok, SHIN Sang-ok is described as follows. Speaking of SHIN's period living with a prostitute, he says, "I have this story about how he did not discriminate in his methods in order to make films. He says how he got close to a prostitute who serviced Westerners. She earned a lot of US dollars, so they lived in one room, and when the US soldiers came in he would hide under the bed. He was so bold telling her to lay down for those Yankee bastards. And with the money he got that way, he was able to keep filming."

I do not feel that the information presented here is of such directly vital importance in understanding the works of SHIN Sang-ok the film director. However, I think it is necessary for an understanding of SHIN Sang-ok the historical figure. This is because he was an all too "Korean" figure who is difficult to understand simply in view of his films.

If you remove the films made by SHIN Sang-ok and Shin Films, Korean film history in the 1960s ends up half empty. Through Shin Films, many outstanding Korean directors were able to make films, and Korean production technology took a step forward. The major films that he directed were satisfactory both in popular terms and judged on their merits as films. SHIN has his quasi-regular actors, like KIM Jin-gyu and CHOI Eun-hee, but he also collaborated well with major actors like KIM Seung-ho, and major Korean stars like SHIN Sung-il got their start at SHIN's hands. Most importantly, SHIN was the first to run a film studio that was like a company and to operate a film lot properly. He himself did not consider 'SHIN Sang-ok the film director' and 'SHIN Sang-ok the producer' separately, and he once recounted how he did not think he would have made better films if he had just worked as a director.[21] He sought to make a Korean Hollywood and to develop a world market. But at the time when he was working, the 1960s in Korea, it was military dictators rather than democracy that reigned supreme, and the priority was economic activity devoted to the issue of immediate survival rather than cultural life. Unreason, absurdity, suppression and the pressures of modernization were unavoidable obstacles not only for the masses but also for individuals involved in film like SHIN Sang-ok. So his desire led him to join forces with powerful figures in politics, and that fortune gave rise to a mistake, and that mistake threw the reality surrounding SHIN into despair. At the moment when he had fallen in despair, he found himself in North Korea.

In South Korea, if someone said that he was dragged to North Korea against his will, he would have to endure the dubious glances of people from the moment he set foot on South Korean soil again. A period of time characterized by a strong

21. SHIN Sang-ok, 2007, p. 20.

"Red Complex" dominated South Korean society until the mid-1990s. Within such a society, SHIN was both a big figure of the past whom nobody could take lightly and an outsider at the same time. And so one could call him a kind of film history in himself, and a system for understanding Korean film. I am not calling him a system merely in the sense of how he operated a large film company in Shin Films, nor in the sense of how he had an individual production system of his own as a filmmaker. It is because the many cinematic realities and the real situation of division that he went through were one of the systems of Korean film that I refer to him as such.

On March 2003, the South Korean presidency was passing from KIM Dae-jung, who opened the road to reconciliation between the two Koreas, to the new president, ROH Moo-hyun. At this time, SHIN published a long letter called "As long as the Republic of Korea survives, I will never forgive you for selling out our people for a Nobel Prize"[22] in the *Monthly Chosun*, a major far-right magazine in South Korea. It was a writing in letter form too long and specialized for one to believe that he wrote it himself, yet at the same time one could not doubt it. Even if someone had written it for him, wouldn't SHIN at least have had to agree with the intent? Did he have some unfathomable sentiments toward KIM Dae-jung, or was he really an anti-Communist deep down in his bones? SHIN called his autobiography *I, Was Film*. Was film really everything there was to life for SHIN Sang-ok, or was it just a means of survival?

22. SHIN Sang-ok, "Last Letter Addressed to President KIM Dae-jung," *Monthly Chosun*, March 2003, pp. 64-80.

Interview

Interview

by LEE Gi-rim

An Explanation for *The Evil Night*

The director SHIN Sang-ok, who first approached the films of CHOI In-kyu as an art direction team member for the Korea Film Association, has a high regard for the films released around the time of Korean independence, as this was the generation that solved technical issues such as "Is this audible? Can you see this?" And in a country reduced to ruins once again by war, he introduced himself to the next generation as someone who dreamed alone of a cinematic art movement.

This interview was conducted in 16 installments by film historian LEE Gi-rim in the Korean film weekly *Cine 21* (2003) and has been compiled by YI Hyo-in.

SHIN: Joining the Korea Film Association, I made *Eve of Independence* and *Sinner Without Sin*, and after that something called *The People's Vote*, a cultural film about how to vote. It was the first example of simultaneous recording in Korean film. Films before that, including *Hurrah! For Freedom*, were all dubbed later. When the Americans occupied Japan, they took a camera called a "Mitchell" to Korea as a war trophy. Of course, they didn't give it away completely; we acquired the one that the US Information Service had, and it was the first film to have simultaneous recording with the Mitchell camera. *Sinner Without Sin* is about some pastor, who won't worship at shrines. In the end, he goes to prison and dies, and the film is his life story.

What I did in art direction was sets. The props and everything, that's all art. And I even did posters. At that time, there wasn't really any specialization, so we fancied ourselves to be specializing. The production staff had cameras, everyone had cameras and carried them around. But I did art, so I just sat there quietly trying not to be seen. One day they stopped, saying that if SHIN Sang-ok didn't go out, they weren't going to go out either, and I ended up having a really hard time. I wondered why I should be carrying machines around when I was doing art.

Anyway, that was the time when I sensed that film wasn't just moving photographs. You know how a painter is always thinking about "esprit"? In the same way, I had the thought that "It should be like this," and I started to say to myself, "This isn't a film, this is a moving photograph." The first film I had after that was *The Evil Night* (1952). It has a similar story with *A Flower in Hell* (1958), a kind of early *A Flower in Hell*, so to speak. Because it's the story of a *yangbuin* (a prostitute catering to foreigners). There was something in a magazine called *Baengmin*, a short piece by KIM Gwang-ju, three or four pages. A man is hit by a car walking on the street one rainy night, a jeep which is the car of a *yangbuin*, and she's a student from the girls' school he used to teach at. She suggests that he go home with her, and she goes through various situations and leaves in the morning. It's a story that takes place over one night. One day I looked and these kids passing by were throwing rocks and yelling, "Foreigner's whore, foreigner's whore." That's the ending, and at the time, when I was young, I liked it so much, it was so moving, so I made the short story into a full-length film. That became my first film, and if it were still around now they might call it the first work of "realism" in Korean film.

In a way, everyone likes their first film the best, and even IM Kwon-taek likes his first film best, whether it was *Farewell to Tuman River* or whatever. I look at my films the same way, and if you ask why, it's because of the compilation of techniques. Because I used all the techniques I had. At that time, we didn't think about box office or anything like that, we just went ahead and filmed whatever we were filming with all our hearts. If it were still around now, it would be interesting in various ways [...] But oddly enough, they say there's still a film called *Piagol* around, which is from the same time period.

As for making *The Evil Night* with the Art Association, it was because at the time what I always had in mind was a cinematic movement, a new movement that wasn't in the name of some individual company. We had a strong sense that we were representing cinematic art, we were that kind of group, so maybe because of that sense we always put names like that on it. The New Theater Association, that was Shinhyeop, right? It's a group that YU Chi-jin made in theater called the Drama and Art Association. So by having a new theater movement, a new cinema movement, we have this Cinema Art Association, even if it's just me. It's an imaginary name. I got all intoxicated by myself and made it. So when the Korean War broke out, we fled, and when the territory was recovered on September 18, there was nowhere to sleep. I went to a bombed-out office, laid out some newspapers on a desk and slept there, and I'm in the ruins thinking about how I had to do a kind of Theatrical Film Art Association. Happy people.

Korea, Dreams

The Cinema Art Association, which made *Korea*(1954), was from the time in the war when I was in an empty house sleeping on a desk and thinking about an art and cinema association, and I was thinking of what you might call a symbolic association, in other words, how we had to get artists together and make independent productions, a kind of "United Artists." So it was total fantasy, when I was very young. What I made thinking that I had to get together not just myself but all independent producers was the Art Association, but it ended up just being a one-off. After that, there was the Seoul Film Company, which carried the name of film company for the first time. I was thinking that we could only make money if we had a film company. There was a kind of office, a single room, me and BYEON Sun-je and some three or four other people. With the Seoul Film Company, we had in mind something more like a kind of distribution company rather than production. I thought that distribution was pretty important, you know? Shin Productions or whatever would have a sense of being about production, and the Seoul Film Company would have the sense of a company that did distribution. So I made the Seoul Film Company with the concept of a distribution company.

In *Korea* there's a bit about the Chun-hyang story, and about the *cheoyongmu* mask dance and Seokguram Grotto, and gathering all of that took a long time. It may have been the first time Seokguram Grotto was filmed for a movie. Going up there, it was all a field of gravel. At that time, if you didn't have a jeep, you couldn't go up there. It was filmed as a documentary so that it could be sold overseas. It was made for people who were ignorant of Korea, so they could get all of its history and present in one glance, and we edited it so that it was easy to watch, with a dramatic narrative structure. It wasn't long, maybe an hour and a half, but we filmed it in 35 mm at a time when in a good year you had maybe one or two films in 35 mm, so in that sense it was quite an accomplishment.

Dreams (1955) wasn't something I did (produced); it was BYEON Sun-je who put the money up for it, and even now I'd like to try doing it again. I liked the story in itself, but it had easy production conditions. Since the time we established an independent film company, expenses had been a problem, sets were a problem and all of that, so the idea that we could basically make it on location, that there were so many locations, actually came to be a good condition. We essentially shot the whole thing in front of the grave of King Sejo, in Gwangneung. We used an Arriflex for the first time, and they said we could only film on Saturday and Sunday, since it was a

stolen Arriflex from the Ministry of Culture and Information.

This was the first version of *Dreams*, done by HWANG Nam, and the second one, starring SHIN Yeong-gyun, was shot in May on Mt. Seorak. The part where the waves come in and all that was Naksan-sa Temple, you know? For the third *Dreams*, I'd like to shoot in somewhere in the South Seas, Thailand or Burma. There are lot of good scenes in *Dreams*, which I hate to have absent artistically. We had a developed formative culture, but nothing strange and totally natural like the monks wearing rubber shoes rather than sandals. During the Joseon dynasty, Buddhism was suppressed, so no matter where you went, there was nothing Buddha-like except the Buddha inside of the Muryangsujeon at Buseok-sa Temple, made during the Goryeo period. Everything was made the same way, made like Chinese ghosts with full stomachs, and there's nothing Buddha-like.

There's a film called *La Perla* (Emilio Fernandez, 1947), based on the book *The Pearl* by John Steinbeck. A Mexican film. The director was famous, but I don't remember his name. A young married couple has a sick child, so for a few days they are unable to go out and catch fish, and then they go out and happen to find a big pearl. A rumor spreads because of the pearl, and they end up being chased by these people who want to steal it. Finally, they throw the pearl in the water, and that's the end. I think *Dreams* was heavily influenced by that film.

Pagoda of No Shadows, A College Woman's Confessions, A Flower in Hell

With *Pagoda of No Shadows*, we couldn't have a spectacle-type film in Korea, so we tried to solve it using a kind of stage setting, and in the end it was a failure. It didn't work with the stage style. At the time, for a while there were a lot of films made in a theatrical style in England, things like Shakespeare plays, *Richard III*. And we couldn't make it feel like Seorabeol (an old name of Gyeongju City) using only sets, so we did it in a stage style, so I guessed you could say we failed because of stubbornness. But even now I think that the story of "Pagoda of No Shadows" is a good subject.

We started having big hits with *Confession* (*A College Woman's Confession*) and *A Flower in Hell*. We probably got audiences because of the title, "A College Woman's Confession." I recall that it was based on a work by Andre Gide, called something like *Betrayal*. At that time, Ms. CHOI (CHOI Eun-hee) was the first out there as a female lawyer, so Dr. LEE Tae-yeong fell in love with her, thought of her as a daughter and treasured her. Wasn't the late LEE Tae-yeong the first female lawyer? And with the prosecutor's argument, we asked MUN In-gu, the real prosecutor to write it and put that in. At that time we had no idea how to do an argument. What did we know?

A Flower in Hell did very good business. I'd sort of done the story of a *yangbuin* beginning with *The Evil Night*, which was my first subject matter. In *A Flower in Hell*, she's a bit active for a *yangbuin*. Actually, it was really something for a woman who seemed a bit more like a bad girl than Ms. CHOI. You couldn't say that she was perfect for the part. At the time, she had established a certain "image" with *Hometown of the Heart*, but she didn't really have that strong an image as the typical Korean woman then. Also, for my part, I needed to make her work a bit. (laughs) So I had her do it. And she was young, so she was in good shape. At the end, the scene in the swamp where Sonya dies was filmed at a stone bridge in front of Hanyang University, the Salgussi Bridge. Everything around was swampland. With *Pagoda of No Shadows*, it wasn't anywhere special either. It's all the Han River.

A Flower in Hell is better known by the French. They recognize it as a major work. So this was the first of our films to have that social quality, since it predated *Aimless Bullet*. What they ask me is whether I've seen *Duel in the Sun* (1946, King Vidor & Otto Brower). That film, starring Joseph Cotten, Jennifer Jones and Gregory Peck, they think I copied it. It has the same story, right, two brothers fighting over a woman? But I'd never seen the film, and the story is completely different.

I saw *A Flower in Hell* for the first time in 40 years in France, and I thought it was well filmed. I guess I was at my wit's end making it because I'd made money with *A College Woman's Confession*, you know? The camera was an IMO, a news camera, and we shot it attaching a 400-foot magazine to the "IMO." The magazine didn't turn, so you had to turn it by hand, which was a real pain. The music was all done with a synthesizer. There's no other music besides the harmonica in it, right? And that's not because I'm great, it's because we had no money. At the time, *The Third Man* (1949, Carol Reed) was all done with a single guitar. "Dangga dangga dang, dangga dangga dang," it's the same tradition. And at that time Italian realism was flourishing for a while. I guess you could say I was influenced by that. Culture is about influencing each other and developing; there's nothing original about it. Just because you're Dan-gun's grandson, it doesn't mean there's a such thing as Dan-gun's culture.

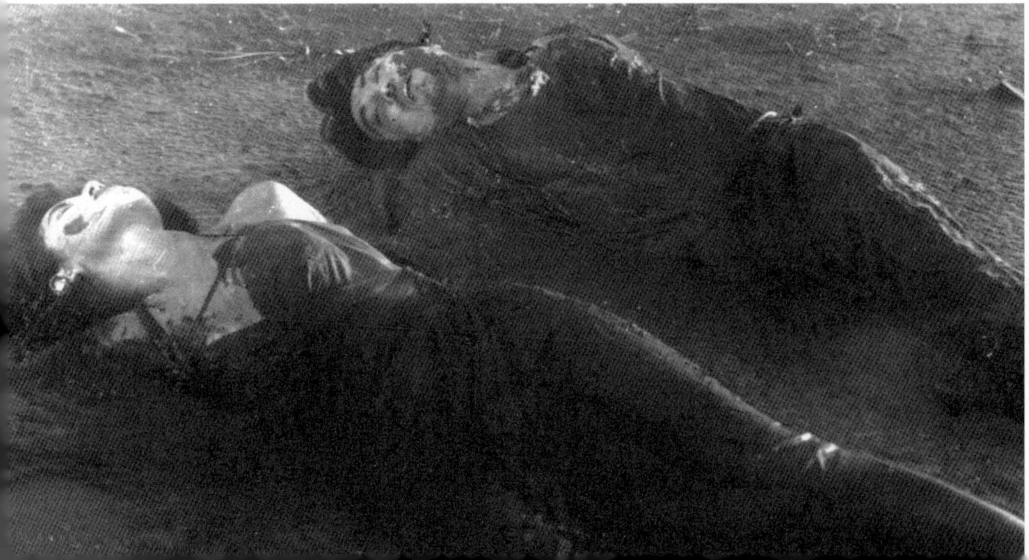

A Flower in Hell, 1958

Dongsimcho, Romance Papa, LEE Seung-man and the Independence Movement, Chun-hie

Dongsimcho wasn't made entirely by me. A producer named PARK Woon-sam brought in the money for it, so I don't have the rights to it yet. And it was based on a hit radio drama, so the film rode that popularity to become a hit. It came to me purely because they wanted Ms. CHOI. At that time, they thought there was no one else to play the role of the widow besides [CHOI Eun-hee], so when they brought the part to her, I had no choice but to direct. The role of Ms. LEE (the war widow played by CHOI Eun-hee) was already imagined that way by everyone listening to the radio. This film was the beginning of my "melodramas."

As for what kind of influence the success of *Dongsimcho*, had, the next film after that was called *The Young LEE Seung-man* (*LEE Seung-man and the Independence Movement*). IM Hwa-su had brought the director LEE Byeong-il in to do it, but it ended up not working, so they'd taken a big hit. It appears that a bodyguard named GWAK in the Blue House had watched all of my films. He said, "SHIN Sang-ok always makes it better than the original," and with him as the main axis I was suddenly pulled away by IM Hwa-su. I had been making *A Sister's Garden* when they took me, and they stopped everything that the other guy had been shooting, and the new film we made was *LEE Seung-man and the Independence Movement*. That was the first film we shot using the Anyang lot. Of course, before that HONG Chan had shot one of his, maybe *Life*, but that was the first time someone from outside came in and really made a big film.

Inside, they built roads and a prison and even a replica of the Independence Gate. I said this at the beginning, but that guy (RHEE Syngman) thought that Korea film was so small because of the machinery, you know? So he brought everything in, automatic developing machines, Mitchell cameras, Westrex recording equipment. But the point is that making a film isn't about machines, it's about minds. So they brought in all this stuff, and we still couldn't do anything. Engineers like LEE Pil-woo (a cinematographer and recording engineer active from the period of the Japanese occupation) came in and ended up failing with the recording on things like *Life*. The recording devices at the Anyang lot were density-type, so it was difficult to do recording or developing. It's a bit easier with area-type. They even had density meters, but it wasn't a time when you could do that. It was too soon. From what I know, the people during the Japanese occupation were all weeded out technically or philosophically after independence and lost their status, and it was because they couldn't overcome that difference in sense. Anyway, the Anyang lot was built to look good for RHEE Syngman, but the films didn't make any money, and even if they lent out the facilities, it wasn't enough to balance the budget. They had interest constantly coming out at the Industrial Bank, and finally they had no choice but to give up. They did that after about 10 years, and I bought it out.

Among my films, *Chun-hie* was made by borrowing the Anyang lot. The film is gone now, so even I never got to see it after I made it. The film was made to make money. At that time, Ms. CHOI's popularity was at its height, and you could

Romance Papa, 1960

say that I made it as a way to cash in. She never really wore anything but hanbok, and Norano saw the "design" and made some pretty good fashion. At that time, Andre KIM had come into the film company wanting to be an actor, and there was no fashion besides Norano. She had hats, and for that time it was pretty novel. Anyway, it was a big hit, since it was a "melodrama."

Romance Papa had an all-star cast for the time. NAMGUNG Won was the son-in-law, SHIN Sung-il was the youngest son, and everyone else, EOM Aeng-ran, DO Geum-bong, KIM Jin-gyu, CHOI Eun-hee, KIM Seung-ho, JU Jeung-nyeo. And JU Seon-tae on top of that. It's a film like nowadays, with a father suffering mistreatment socially, so it got a good reception among the middle-aged.

Madam White Snake

Madam White Snake was taken from a Chinese story. It's in the English title too, isn't it? In Hong Kong too, they did a Japanese co-production called *Madam White Snake*, which was beautiful, but not as good as ours. At that time, we never did any collaborations with Hong Kong, just with each other, and considering that it had some nice artwork. Generally, when Koreans do a Chinese story, they paint strange things on their heads and wrap them in accessories, but for this they used Chinese historical data and made it close to Chinese clothing. The trick photography is different from what they do now, and it's a bit childish, but for what it was [...] We couldn't do optical effects, we couldn't do computer graphics, we couldn't do anything then, you know?

For the part where the Goddess of Mercy is speaking from the heavens, we drilled a hole in a mirror, and the part with no hole was the light of the rest of the sky, and the drilled part was where the Goddess of Mercy came out. For something like the clouds flowing out of the sky, we filled a tank with water and the camera shot from here, the people moved behind, and if you poured India ink in the tank it flowed and looked like clouds. In that kind of way, it was almost primitive, but it looked plausible.

If I talk about this now, you won't really know what I'm talking about, but for example we had the woman standing in a place about this high. (The director draws a picture to show the scene of the filming.) So when the camera shoots from over here, we put the mirror next to the camera and drill the hole like this, you see? The woman appears through the hole, but the part that isn't drilled is all a reflection of the sky. So it looks like someone is floating in the air. That's how it was when the Goddess of Mercy appears. A kind of "mirror work." I recall that we were the first to do that. There was nothing like that in any other film. Using piano wire like that may have been the first time, on stage or screen, since it was the first time I found out about piano wire as well. We used black paint and raised her up so that as much as possible you couldn't see it, and she wore a kind of "corset," like a band around her waist.

It'll pass if you're desperate. Looking at it now it's a marvel, and it's gotten easier, so nowadays nobody would think of that kind of thing. But at that time, we didn't have the resources. With *Pagoda of No Shadows*, which I talked about before, I liked it, but we didn't have the capabilities to shoot it in Korea. It didn't work, not at that time. We had no set, and if you just go to Bulguk-sa Temple and film there, it's a pitch-black pagoda, and there's no way it's going to come out right. We didn't have the capabilities to recreate a Silla era building, and we were just fumbling in the dark. So we ended up shooting in a theatrical

Madam White Snake, 1960

Madam White Snake, 1960

style, like "Act 1, Scene 1," and I liked it because I started out in formative arts, so we tried that, but doing that in itself was a reckless plan. If you look at HYEON Jin-geon's novel (*Pagoda of No Shadows* is based on a novel by HYEON Jin-geon), there's stuff about loving the country in every line, and the concerns of the artist are in the background, and I like that kind of theme. When I was young, I read what was serialized in the Dong-a Ilbo newspaper, and so there's probably a whiff of that too. Nowadays, it might be nice to do it one time, but its chances at the box office wouldn't be good. That's because it's got the story of Asanyeo and the story of Guseul-agi, and they flow as two strands before combining. It's an OK film, but the box office prospects wouldn't be good.

In a sense, the absolute factor in box office is the story. Of course, you need good details too, but the basis is the story. I've tried a few times to watch *Love Me Once Again*. It played a decisive role as a melodrama in Korea, and I thought I could also get a sense of the Korean public's feelings, so I really needed to see it. But I couldn't watch it. The camera isn't even news quality, and I watched for 10 minutes before giving up. If I say this, I might take some flack for it, but there are only actors. The camera is a mess. Looking at that, box office is all about the story, and not about things like whether it's well shot or comes out looking good.

SEONG Chun-hyang

The Seoul Film Company was something idea-driven. I thought that I needed to do distribution, so I went ahead and did it. Nowadays we do distribution, production and everything, but in the old days the distribution companies were separate. And on top of that it was a way of doing things where you sold off the rights. But we had no power or capital, so the distribution failed and we ended up starting production work.

And as for it having the image of a production company, that was all after *Chun-hyang* (*SEONG Chun-hyang*). Before that, we had staff that we worked with, but we only used salaried, fixed staff members after *Chun-hyang*. At that time, I was running Shin Films, or maybe Shin Productions, in Choong-dong. I did recruiting for newcomers, and some 3,000 people came. None of them were usable, so I didn't pick anyone except (SHIN) Sung-il, and it was the same as doing recruiting at KBS today. We didn't have anything like television then, you know? Besides films. Films, image media, ruled everything at the time.

From the time after *Chun-hyang* to the time when we quit the Anyang lot, we had around 250 employees, since DO Geum-bong, NAMGUNG Won, HEO Jang-gang, KIM Seung-ho, SHIN Sung-il and SHIN Yeong-gyun were all at their peak. The exclusive contracts weren't there to prevent them from working for other people, it was because we were filming three movies a month, so there was no choice at all but to have house actors. You couldn't just let them go around. It takes more than two months to do one film, so you had to film five movies at the same time in one month for two to come out. Here is where there's a divide between Chungmuro and Shin Films. At Chungmuro, they have "independents," and as Shin Films grew it started to become a force that clashed with Chungmuro. You see, at the time, after *Chun-hyang* I thought that film had possibilities as an industry and I industrialized it.

With everything, film history or cultural history, there's a starting point like in Greece or Egypt, and as you go along it widens into a zenith, then tapers off, and you turn around and it seems like it's growing again. Film is the same way. At the beginning, I was an independent, and then finally a "major," and it's because you had to be a major to have the facilities necessary to shoot everything. I went as a major, and then back to being an independent. To put it simply, it's nice to work as an independent with a creator's mentality, but if you do that you can't make films. You can't shoot what you want to. So I think that it was because I showed the possibilities of film as an industry that the big conglomerates also started to get involved in film.

Film laws came about after the coup in 1961. With film companies, you had so many bankruptcies and people fleeing and everything. They drew up these artificial sanctions, like a studio had to be so many square meters, it had to have so many cameras, it had to make so many films a year. But it isn't something that can be solved by artificial means. I wasn't able to make more than three films even with the big facilities at the Anyang lot, so how were they supposed to make more than three a year with a tiny warehouse? The film laws had many fundamental problems. You can say that they had no practical effects.

Some people think that because I had a big film studio I made laws so that people without them couldn't make films, that I suppressed them, but that's not true at all. Film laws were entirely the idea of the soldiers. At first, I stayed away from the laws. I did become close to PARK Chung-hee because of *Evergreen Tree*. He said that he cried after watching it. After that was the start of the Evergeen movement and the Saemaeul movements, and because of that we grew closer, and then there was the selloff of the Anyang lot. That's how you can look at it.

The Birth of Shin Films

At that time, there were maybe 100 or so film companies, something like that? Everybody said "I can make a film" and all went out to make movies. There were a lot of unsavory incidents that occurred as side effects from the "independent" movement. Because film is gambling, people ran off without making the film, things like that, or if the film went bust they would disappear. The military government, they were the ones who thought, "That won't do, we have to fix it." And so they reorganized the film companies. But you have to view it as a myopic policy. I talked about this before, but just because you have facilities, it doesn't mean you can make films.

After their reorganization, there were maybe 16 or so film companies, and the contradictory part was that there were so many side effects, since they didn't do the research all at once. You had equipment going here and there, and all you had to do was rent a warehouse and you had a had a 200 *pyeong* (approximately 660 square meter) studio. The 200-*pyeong* standard was so vague that it was enough just to have 200 pyeong, with no standards, regardless of whether it was soundproofed or if you could even shoot there. It was total trial and error.

The offices for Shin Film were in what was then the Dongmyeong Building in Seoul. What's sitting there now? It was there, and the studio (Wonhyo-ro studio) was in the place of the old Dongyang Bakery factory. It was a huge warehouse that even had a railroad in it, and we and Dongyang Bakery were together on the two sides of the railroad. The facilities were about ten cameras, since they weren't simultaneous recording cameras, so they weren't expensive. Simultaneous recording was difficult there, because of the sound of the train. You couldn't do it anywhere but the Anyang lot. We also had one or two zoom lenses. They were called "knock," mainly made in Japan, which we bought and used here. *Romance Gray* may have been where we really started using zoom lenses. Before that, there may not have been any zoom lenses in Korean film.

At the time of *SEONG Chun-hyang*, we were shooting in Cinemascope, so we bought some German lenses called "Ultrascope" and used those, and the day for night technique was first used on *Prince Yeonsan*. At that time, there was a lot of discussion of the issue of how to shoot natural colors as a technical issue. So, we used the technique of shooting day for night, or what have you. Overall, we didn't really know how to shoot night scenes in the day. At those times, there was no way to reflect all of the light, so we generally shot night scenes using sunlight. What we usually used was Kodak film, so we used a lot of special techniques suited to the properties of Kodak film. That kind of this is peculiar in a technical sense, but since we had a company it was OK. It would have been too much for an individual to do.

As for Shin Films becoming an enterprise and making lots of films, you can look at it this way. It was like a pyramid. For example, for one film to come out, you had to shoot two, and to shoot two you needed four actors. So in that way, for one film to come out, the bottom would get larger and larger. The situation was one where you had to start by attaching one screenwriter to one (star-level) actor. At that time DO Geum-bong was under an exclusive contract, all the actors were

Romance Gray, 1963

under exclusive contracts, and they had their own ambitions too, so you would just have to film in a way suited to that, right?

Not just the actors, the screenwriters too were all under exclusive contracts. IM Hee-jae, KIM Gang-yun, GWAK Il-lo, people like that. IM Hee-jae wrote *My Mother and Her Guest* and *SEONG Chun-hyang*, and was a good writer. KIM Gang-yun wrote *Evergreen Tree*. In addition, there was LEE Sang-hyeon, a fellow named IM Chun-hui, and LEE Hee-woo, who wrote *Deogi* (a television drama), and it was mainly those people working.

With direction, it's a kind of subcontracting, where they bring in works themselves, or we support them. A lot of directors—LEE Man-hee, LEE Hyeong-pyo, KIM Su-yong—all did it that way. IM Won-sik, who's in the Korea Film Directors' Society now, and KIM Su-dong, who's like a godfather of television, they were directors at that time.

Shin Films and Chungmuro

After we became an enterprise, Shin Films and Chungmuro grew apart. You could call it a two-peaked mountain range. The Manchurian plain action films that people like JEONG Chang-hwa and CHOI Wan-gyu did, we didn't do that kind of thing, you know? We did purely nationwide stuff, things with pretensions of art. From their end, it must have looked like we were totally playing in an ivory tower. But the independents weren't healthy independents, they were doing things purely to pay their credits, so they had no choice but to shoot whichever way they were forced to. That's how film is, you know? In "capitalism" in particular, you have to use popular actors, or you have to make melodramas this time because "melodrama" worked in the old days. In that sense, they're films made by the people with the money, and you couldn't really view them as films made by the producers.

This is how Shin Films was set up. The production staff members and director doubled as producers. They'd do the budget and said, "How much can we do it for? How much will it cost?" and then contract it out. In general, you could think of it as director-centered subcontracting. But it was screwed up in the organization and ultimately couldn't really make money, and the quality of the films began to drop, because they kept doing the "in my pocket" thing. The producers are supposed to stay aware and bring money in where it's needed, but some directors kept taking a cut and didn't put the money into the production costs. The mass production system was messed up. The film business itself didn't have the capacity for mass production. They rushed into it too much. Film is something that you have to coax and fiddle with and develop piece by piece, and it wasn't going to work shoving it around like a foster child, not really.

When it came time to decide on a film, there was something called a planning room. What the planning room produced you just took as a reference. But they didn't have anything like the scientific research you have today; it was more like, "It worked this way, so let's do it this way." HWANG Ki-sung, of the HWANG Ki-sung Corporation today, was director, and the late GANG Geun-sik, some other people were in the planning room. Every year I would do one or two films I wanted to. I was the only one who had his own company and could do whatever he wanted. Other people all gave theirs and we would do it that way.

The funding was all done by regional entertainment companies who came in, selling "the rice before the harvest and taking the profits," but my films didn't really have any difficulties, because in general they made a lot of money. You couldn't call them blockbusters—even if you put a lot of money into it, you wouldn't draw that many people—but I hadn't made mistakes commercially, so they trusted me and bought them. In cases like *Deaf Samryong-i*, it didn't make money even when NA Woon-gyu did it, and they brought one in from China called *The Bride and the Deaf Man*, but it was a failure too, so it was just ours. Because of that kind of situation, there were many cases where I thought that even if we suffered a lot on other things, there would be money left over from my stuff, so we took those. At that time, well, all we had to do was show our trailers and the others would all run.

With the advertising, we did the trailers, and the main advertising was done at the theaters. And the entertainment companies too did a bit of advertising. Maybe two weeks before we went into the theaters they would do it there. So there were times when we didn't stamp the name of the theater beforehand in our advertising, and the theater paid once they put the name on it. At that time most of the advertisements were in the newspapers, and I don't think we really did any on TV. It wasn't very widespread, and it was in black-and-white, so television was meaningless. But there was a phenomenon then where they kind of hated Shin Films in mass communication. It's like that now too, but I couldn't really handle the reporters. At that time, there were not many films, but there were film magazines coming out, and each newspaper had film reporters. In Korea, there were not many films, and I thought, "What use is there with all these reporters?" and wouldn't meet them. I think that's the reason my films never got much praise. When I think about it now it was a necessary evil, but at the time I didn't meet them out of that feeling.

The Management Strategy and Limitations of Shin Films

Like I mentioned before, with block booking, exclusive theaters showed only your movies and nobody else's, and Myeongbo Theater was one of Shin Films' exclusive theaters. At that time, you didn't need anything like an exclusive theater if you had a good film. If you had something good, the theaters would just follow you. So these exclusive theaters appeared. The regional entertainment companies made them and asked us to make two films a month.

The problem was that what I invested didn't match up with the money coming up from the provinces. What we sold them was 20 million won, and the production costs would be 25 million won, like that. We didn't do the business right. That's how narrow the market was and how much production costs went in, you could say. The ones that cost a lot where mainly mine, the historical pieces and whatnot [...] At that time, we had no choice, so we did it that way.

It would have been better if we'd invested in real estate (theaters). In the future, they would have their own line of theaters in the Japanese styles, and the theaters would do it directly as well, but that kind of thing would only work for the future, and at the time there was no money so I didn't get involved. If you're going to do screening, you need a huge network. And at the time, if you didn't want to pay tax, and you sold 100 tickets, you would tell them you only sold 50, and they couldn't check. If they sent someone to stand out there to watch, you would buy that person off too. There was no oversight at all. Later, we did something called the Hollywood Theater, which was the first theater I made. But I would have to say that I wasn't really involved in it at all. At the time, I should have invested a little in real estate (theaters), but I couldn't. So I ended up with financial difficulties. In Japan as well, the companies that only made movies and didn't invest in real estate were the first to fail. Take Daiei, which made *Rashomon*.

When we sold it to the provinces, it would be one for Daegu, one for Busan, the Honam Line (North and South Jeolla Provinces) were counted as one, Gyeonggi Province and Chungcheong Province. Maybe those five? Jeju-do would have been done in South Gyeongsang Province. Or maybe it was the Honam Line? Jeju-do was so tiny at the time. Things like *Simcheong* did well in the Honam area, but didn't really bring people in in Yeongdong and Yeongnam. In rare cases, something that worked in Seoul didn't work in the provinces, and things that worked in the provinces didn't work in Seoul. That was generally the case with the "shinpa"-style melodramas. I did a total of three *Simcheong* films, one in Korea that I gave to someone else to make (LEE Hyeong-pyo's *Dae Simcheong-jeon*), one I did (*Hyonyeo Simcheong*, and one I did in the North. *Simcheong* wasn't "shinpa," but it seems like it suited the Honam audiences, oddly enough. Generally, what was a hit in Seoul was a hit in the provinces too, and it was the case with things like *Deaf Samryong-i* that had a popular quality and an artistic quality as well. But anything with only artistry and no popular quality may have worked in Seoul but it wouldn't work in the provinces at all. In that sense, the only people who combined both sides would have been, what, LEE Man-hee and KIM Ki-young? That's the principle of film. Without those two wheels, it doesn't go.

Later we would split the company into various parts. The reason was that the film laws had quotas for the films a company produced. It didn't matter with one company, but if you wanted a large quota, in other words if you wanted to make a lot of films, you had to have a lot of film companies, right? So, since our studio was big, we divided it into various parts and registered them. Shin-a Films, Anyang Films, Star Films, those names all come from that. When you think about it now it's ridiculous, but that's the production quota distribution, where they said "one company should only make so many films." But you can't do it that way, so the administration doesn't work. So we did it under various names. As for Shin Films' peak, I don't know, maybe it would have to be when we made *Prince Daewon* (1968, Anyang Films production). When we did simultaneous recording. Before that, there were things like *Box of Death*, but in the sense of being something produced entirely by our own hands, it was really *Prince Daewon* that was Korea's first simultaneous recording.

Biography

Biography

SHIN Sang-sok was born in 1926 in Cheongjin, North Hamgyeong Province, the youngest of five children to father SHIN Byeong-yong and mother KIM Bong-seon. His original name was SHIN Tae-seo; SHIN Sang-ok is a name that he used when working in film. His father was a noted doctor of Chinese medicine in the region and would die during the evacuation period of the Korean War.

During his time at Cheonma Normal School, he enjoyed going to the theater, and he received his influences while watching the films of NA Woon-gyu, who in 1925 made *Arirang*, a legendary work in Korean cinema, as well as those of Charlie Chaplin, European and American films, and the Japanese samurai film *Chanbara* (the title is a compound made from "chan chan," the sound of clashing swords, and "bara bara," the sound of blood spattering). He was so enthusiastic about the cinematic medium that he once bought a hand-operated projector without his father's knowledge and used it to watch old films until it caught fire and the projector burned up completely. The films he recalled from that time included Chaplin's *Modern Times*, *The Gold Rush* and *The Great Dictator*, NA

Woon-gyu's *Arirang*, LEE Gyu-hwan's *The Ownerless Ferryboat* and *Vagabond*, and D.W. Griffiths' *The Birth of a Nation* and *The Last Days of Pompeii.*

Following his graduation from Cheonma Normal School, he became engrossed in film and painting at Gyeongseong Middle School, a five-year school that had the highest reputation in Cheongjin. He spent his middle school years in an environment where a literary atmosphere flourished under the influence of his Korean teacher KIM Ki-rim, a pioneering modernist poet in the Joseon literary world, and his art teacher KIM Ha-geon, who had graduated from the Tokyo University of the Arts. His classmates included the animator SHIN Dong-heon, a pioneering director in Korean animation; the poet KIM Gyu-dong; and KIM Cheol, a politician who would be appointed leader of the Korean Socialist Party. In his second year of middle school, a time when he was serving as head of the art class and was fascinated by surrealism, he became a major topic of discussion when he was selected for the Seonjeon, the top gateway to success in the art world, sponsored by the Japanese Governor-General of Korea during the occupation of Korea. The time that followed was a chaotic one, as the school changed from a five-year system to a four-year one and the students were called away as conscripts for the Japanese army, so four-year graduates also left to study in Japan.

In 1944, he matriculated at the Tokyo University of the Arts in Ueno. At the time, the style of French surrealism was the rage, and SHIN guessed that this may have been connected with a spirit of resistance toward the militarism that has led to the war. He was enthusiastic about film as well as art, impressed by the works of directors such as Marcel Carnet and Julien Duvivier, and the French coloring that came into SHIN's films is said to have been influenced by this time. He recalled his art studies as a good training in identifying the essence hidden within objects, drawing it out and forming it in a visible way. But he did not finish his art studies, returning to Korea in April 1945, and greeted Korea's liberation from Japan on August 15 of that year just as he was worrying about evading the draft.

Following the liberation, he painted posters for the American Military Government Office to earn a living and ended up painting film posters as well. After seeing CHOI In-kyu's *Hurrah! For Freedom* (1946), he came to work under

CHOI through the intercession of his brother, SHIN Tae-seon, making sets and shooting stills, but he endured great difficulties because of the low wages, which were insufficient for a basic livelihood. SHIN recalled that, if he learned the basics of film and the filmmaker's spirit from NA Woon-gyu, he learned the core technique of real filmmaking from CHOI In-kyu. He would say that his performing of duties not only of direction but also cinematography and editing was due to the influence of the almighty technician that was CHOI. After serving as assistant director on CHOI's *Eve of Independence* (1948), SHIN would come to work independently.

In 1950, he would make his debut as a director with *The Evil Night* (1952), a film based on the short novel *Agya* by KIM Gwang-ju. He had originally planned to go to Japan to work, but he ran up against opposition within his home, and his situation was one where he could not go to Japan even if he received support for production costs. War broke out during filming, so SHIN packed up the film and took it down to Busan to complete it and hold the premiere. The film was shot on film obtained with some difficulty from the American forces, so the image quality was rough, and one of the leading directors in Korean film, YU Hyun-mok, director of *Aimless Bullet* (1961), worked as assistant director. SHIN grew to dislike the life of sharing one room with many family members during the evacuation period, so he spent six months living with a *yangbuin* (a prostitute who catered to foreign clients), and he recalled how this provided great help in the making of this film. Later, he joined the military as a member of the Air Force Troop Information photography team, producing an Air Force film entitled *Sortie Order* with director HONG Seong-gi and guaranteeing his standing. While seeking refuge, his father was killed in a bombing attack, and his mother too died during the evacuation.

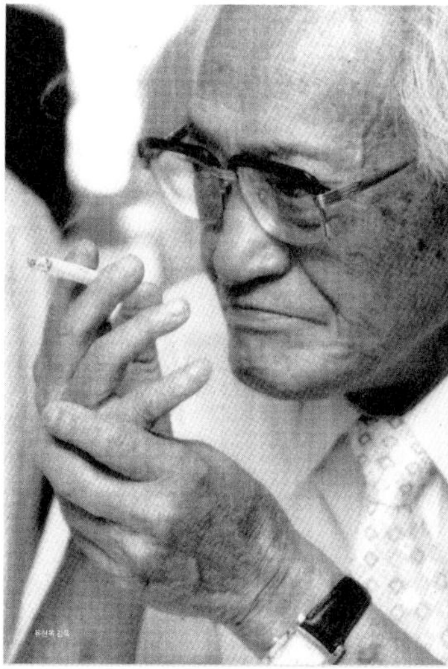
YU Hyun-mok

A College Woman's Confession, 1958

In 1954, at the time of the making of the semi-documentary *Korea* (1954), he met the actress CHOI Eun-hee, who would become his wife and work with him until the end. At the time, CHOI was separated from her first husband, cinematographer KIM Hak-seong; a public controversy would follow widespread reports in the media about KIM's accusations of adultery. But because KIM and CHOI had not formally reported their marriage, no legal problems would occur.

In 1958, SHIN registered a major box office success with *A College Woman's Confession*, starring CHOI, ensuring for himself a favorable social position and confidence in film, and he enjoyed enough financial stability to pay back all of the debts he had incurred making films and then some, as well as to make four melodramas the following year, including *Chun-hie*. The idea for this film was taken from the French film *Betrayal*, and it was also filmed in Japan under the title of *A Female Lawyer's Confession*.

In 1959, SHIN would make *LEE Seung-man and the Independence Movement*. The film was made for use in the election of then-President RHEE Syngman, who was running for office again, and production duties were handed by the anti-communist youth brigade of IM Hwa-su, famous as a political thug, while Chief Bodyguard GWAK Yeong-ju of the Blue House provided support behind the scenes. Virtually all people in film were mobilized for the making of this project, which generated a lot of discussion, and during the making of it the popular actor KIM Hui-gap was struck while standing up to IM Hwa-su, resulting in a fractured rib. SHIN left the film he had been making to work on this project, but he would recall that he did not feel forced to do so, while saying it was an incident that proved how powerless artists were in the face of power and money. Rather, the film became an opportunity for him to enjoy the possibilities of and gain

Prince Daewon

confidence from a project at a large scale, and it would provide support in the making of later historical films such as *Prince Daewon*.

In 1960, he established the film company Shin Films and made *Romance Papa*, which would become both a representative work for him and provide the foundation for later operations of Shin Films.

1961's *My Mother and Her Guest*, considered one of his principal works, would win him the award for Best Film at the first annual Grand Bell Awards. In the same year, he enjoyed a great box office success with *SEONG Chun-hyang*. The film was made with SHIN's wife, CHOI Eun-hee, in the lead, in response to rival director HONG Seong-gi's film on the same story, *The Story of Chun-hyang*, which started HONG's wife KIM Ji, and was a great critical and commercial success. Later, South Korean film studios would be merged and abolished in the name of management rationalization by the PARK Chung-hee administration, and Shin Films was re-registered in 1962.

In 1963, on his third appointment, he took over as chairman of the Korean Film Workers Association, subsequently serving three terms.

In 1964, he won the Best Director prize at the 11th annual Asia Film Festival with *Red Muffler*. Running the company became difficult because of a financial deficit related to the operation of Shin Films, but the system was maintained intact.

In 1967, he took over the filming lot at Anyang, the largest in Asia with an area of 25,000 *pyeong* (approx. 82,645 square meters) and equipped with the highest quality facilities, including Mitchell cameras. With the help of Prime Minister KIM Jong-pil, he took over a lot that had basically turned into ruins, with facilities that people in film had not often been able to take advantage of, and this would provide an opportunity to begin a system of mass production, making some 28 films a year with a staff of more than 30 directors and more than 250 salaried employees. Also, he opened the Anyang Academy of Cinema and Art in 1967, a formal school formed by expanding the Shin Films acting studio that he had run before then. The school would operate for the next 10 years or so until 1978, when his wife CHOI Eun-hee was abducted to North Korea.

In 1969, he received the Best Director prize at the 15th Asia Film Festival for *Women of the Joseon Dynasty*.

In 1970, he won the Best Director prize at Spain's Sitges Film Festival for *A Thousand Year Old Fox*.

In 1975, his film company license was revoked following the insertion in the trailer for his film *The Rose and the Wild Dog* of a scene deleted by censors. This was a measure of retaliation against Shin Films realized as its relationship with the PARK Chung-hee administration deteriorated after having maintained a good relationship and provided direct and

A Thousand Year Old Fox, 1969

The Rose and the Wild Dog, 1975

indirect support. SHIN would claim that it originated from various statements of protest related to film censorship and from personal issues (a scandal related to his adulterous relationship with actress OH Su-mi). As the 1970s went on, the curtain came down on the heyday of Shin Films, and its management situation would grow continually worse from then on, while SHIN and his wife CHOI Eun-hee would eventually divorce in 1976 over his relationship with OH.

On January 14, 1978, CHOI was abducted by North Korean agents, and six months later SHIN too was kidnapped. For the following year, SHIN would make several escape attempts, but was discovered and sentenced to prison before reuniting with CHOI five years later.

In 1983, a Shin Films production lot was constructed in North Korea through the special consideration of KIM Jong-il; SHIN was appointed its president and CHOI its vice-president. There, they would make seven films directly, including *The Secret Envoy Who Never Returned*, while producing more than ten North Korean films at the lot, including *Road*. The Shin Films production lot was equipped with the largest facilities in East Asia at over 20,000 *pyeong* (1 *pyeong* is roughly equal to 3.3 square meters) in total floor space, including two studios of 400 *pyeong* in downtown Pyeongyang, two studios of 200 *pyeong*, six recording rooms and five theaters/projection rooms.

On March 13, 1986, SHIN Sang-ok and CHOI Eun-hee succeeded in a

Mayumi, 1990

dramatic escape in Vienna, Austria, seeking refuge in the United States. That year, the two would reaffirm their wedding vows in the United States and begin living under protection from the US CIA.

In 1990, he began work on *Genghis Khan*, which had long been conceiving since his time in North Korea, with a promise of 30 million US dollars in support from a Japanese man named Hirano. Filming began with a script by John Briley, the screenwriter for *Gandhi*, but when the Japanese economic situation deteriorated filming was interrupted. During this time, SHIN made *Mayumi* under the production of Japan's Tokyo Broadcasting.

In 1991, he established an independent production company, Sheen Productions, in Hollywood, and produced a commercially-focused children's film called *3 Ninjas* for US$3 million, with Jon Turteltaub as director. Distributed by Disney, the film was a big hit, ranking 6th at the box office. Later, more films would be made in the series.

In 1994, he made *Vanished*, which dealt with the disappearance of PARK Chung-hee era Korean CIA director KIM Hyung-wook. The film was conceived after SHIN read the first book shown to him by North Korea's KIM Jong-il, KIM Hyung-wook's ghost-written *Power and Conspiracy*. With this film, SHIN was invited as a jury member for the Cannes Film Festival, and *Vanished* was given a special screening. Later, he would be chief of the judging committee for the Bucheon Fantastic Film Festival and engage in international activities such as lead judge for France's Deauville Asian Film Festival, while receiving a new assessment through countless retrospectives and special exhibitions, including retrospectives at the Pusan International Film Festival and the United States' Museum of Modern Art (MOMA).

In March 2003, he established the Shin Film Art Center, following the Anyang Cinema and Art School, but for various administrative reasons it suffered hardships and financial difficulties.

In 2004, he served as general director for the musical *Crazy for You* and was appointed honorary professor for the Dong-ah Institute of Media and Arts.

On April 11, 2006, following two surgical operations, he succumbed to liver cancer and passed away.

Synopsis

Synopsis

The Evil Night (1952)

A poor writer, unable to pay his rent, goes to collect payment from a magazine company, but fails to do so and ends up drinking heavily with a friend. On his way home, he is struck by a car in which a prostitute is riding; the prostitute had been his student. Because there is a curfew, he sleeps at the prostitute's house, but there is a lot of noise as American soldiers, and even the woman's ex-husband, come to visit. There is a crying child in the closet, whom the man pacifies with chocolate. Meanwhile, the writer's wife, chased out for being unable to pay the rent, moves by herself to the neighborhood where the prostitute lives and happens to see her husband coming out of the woman's house. The writer gets angry and moves to another neighborhood.

---

* This does not cover the entire filmography of SHIN Sang-ok.

** As a rule, synopses were written so that one can get a basic sense of what the story of each film is, and have been modified based on data listed in the Korean Film Archive's KMDB.

Korea (1954)

Semi-documentary mixture of documentary footage and dramatized segments. A full-length culture piece that introduces the characteristic ways of life in various scenic locations in Korea together with dramatized segments depicting the ancient history of those locations.

Dreams (1955)

The young Buddhist monk Jo-sin is captivated by the beauty of Dallye, daughter of the governor-general, but she marries a man from the aristocracy. Jo-sin shares a romance with her even after this before suffering vengeance at the hands of her husband. In the end, all is revealed to have been Dreams.

The Youth (1955)

The late Joseon era. AN Jae-yeong (CHOE Mu-ryong), who has lost his parents because of the villainous minister MIN Gyeom-ho, has been betrothed since a young age to LEE In-hwa (CHOI Eun-hee), who is disguising herself as a man and concealing her identity. They join up with other concerned and passionate youths under the leadership of Hwal-min, supported by Prince Daewon, and battle MIN and his confederates. But there is a surprise attack by MIN and his followers. Hwal-min and his cohorts lose their lives, and Jae-young is shot in a fierce battle with MIN, ultimately dying in In-hwa's arms.

Pagoda of No Shadows (1957)

It is the 10th year in the reign of Silla's King Gyeongdeok, on the anniversary of the birth of Buddha. Guseul-agi (CHOI Eun-hee), daughter of Yu-jong, travels with a party to Bulguk-sa Temple, where she meets Asadal (GWAK Geon), a stonemason from Buyeo. Attracted to him, Guseul-agi goes to visit him the next day at the site where he is working on a stone statue of Buddha and discovers Asadal collapsed from exhaustion. While she nurses him back to health, Guseul-agi's feelings for him grow gradually deeper, but he deeply misses his wife Asanyeo (HAN Eun-jin), whom he has left behind in Buyeo. There, Asanyeo waits only for her husband to return, but when her sickly father dies, she goes to Bulguk-sa to find Asadal. But when she comes to believe that his feelings have changed, Asanyeo throws herself into the Shadow Pond and drowns.

A College Woman's Confession (1958)

CHOE So-yeong (CHOI Eun-hee) is a college student majoring in law and living in an unfortunate environment. When the grandmother who paid her tuition dies, So-yeong is faced with the inability to cover her tuition. With the help of a sympathetic performance given by her friend Hui-suk (KIM Suk-il), who dreams of becoming a novelist, So-yeong pretends to be the daughter of National Assemblyman CHOE Rim (KIM Seung-ho) and goes to live at his house. She studies hard and becomes a lawyer. Her first case is the defense of a female prisoner (HWANG Jeong-sun) whose past is coincidentally similar to her own. As she defends her client, So-yeong gives a powerful argument about how difficult it is for a weak woman to survive in a cold capitalist society, drawing tears with her claims for women's rights. Successfully concluding her defense, So-yeong goes home and confesses her own guilt to CHOE Rim's wife (YU Gye-seon).

A Flower in Hell (1958)

Yeong-sik (KIM Hak) and his friends, who live in a village of prostitutes who cater to Westerners, rob the warehouse of the American troops and sell the goods on the market. Yeong-sik's younger brother Dong-sik (CHO Hae-won) comes to Seoul looking for Yeong-sik, finding him in a market street, and goes to the prostitutes' village. Dong-sik tries to get Yeong-sik to come with him back to the country, where their mother lives, but Yeong-sik tells his brother to leave first, and tells Sonya (CHOI Eun-hee) that if he pulls off a big job the two of them can go down into the country and get married. Meanwhile, Sonya has feelings for Dong-sik, and on the night of a dance party, she seduces Dong-sik while Yeong-sik and his friends are out stealing. Sonya and Dong-sik have a secret meeting on the riverside but are found out by Yeong-sik. Yeong-sik and his cohorts leave to rob an American transport train. Planning to flee with Dong-sik, Sonya reports Yeong-sik to the military police. As Yeong-sik is being pursued by them, his truck flips after a gun battle and he narrowly escapes. Sonya, who has come after him, is stabbed by Yeong-sik, who dies of a gunshot wounds after telling Dong-sik to take care of their mother. Dong-sik leaves for the country with Judy (GANG Seon-hui), a prostitute who wants to marry him.

Dongsimcho (1959)

Eight years after losing her husband at the outbreak of the Korean War, LEE Suk-hui (CHOI Eun-hee) is incurring debts running a dress shop. As KIM Sang-gyu (KIM Jin-gyu), director at a publishing company, helps her with her debts, the two of them fall in love. But he is engaged to his boss's daughter, Ok-ju (DO Geum-bong), and his older sister (JU Jeung-nyeo) is speeding the marriage along to help with his career advancement. Suk-hui's grown daughter Gyeong-hui (EOM Aeng-ran) recommends that her mother remarry with Sang-gyu for happiness, but Suk-hui feels conflicted because of the social practices and ethical values placed upon her. She and Sang-gyu truly love each other, but Suk-hui chooses to leave him, sell her home in Seoul and return to her hometown. Bedridden with illness, Sang-gyu hears the news and rushes to Seoul Station, where he watches in torment as the train leaves with Suk-hui on it.

LEE Seung-man and the Independence Movement (1959)

Depicts the young LEE Seung-man (RHEE Syngman), burning with patriotic spirit, heroically engaging in various trailblazing activities, including publishing a newspaper as a main member of the "Independence Association." This project was planned in order to continue the RHEE Syngman presidency.

A Sister's Garden (1959)

Dr. NAM, a father of two daughters, leaves a final instruction for older daughter Jeong-hui (CHOI Eun-hee) to marry the artist Dong-su (NAMGUNG Won) before dying. Because of the father's debts, the family is in danger of losing the house, but the young doctor Sun-cheol (KIM Seok-hun), who attended college thanks to Dr. NAM's help, sells his own house to help Jeong-hui. Sun-cheol loves Jeong-hui, but because of NAM's deathbed instructions he cannot confess his feelings. Jeong-hui goes to look for a job to support the household, and Mr. BANG (KIM Seung-ho), whose illness was cured thanks to Dr. NAM, recommends the position of manager at a *gisaeng* house to Jeong-hui. Meanwhile, younger sister Myeong-hui's (CHOE Ji-hui) feelings for Dong-su develop into love, and the two of them pledge to marry. Jeong-hui wishes the two of them happiness and takes the job managing the gisaeng house. Mr. BANG proposes to Jeong-hui, and she intends to accept, but Sun-cheol confesses his love for her. Realizing his feelings, she leaves Mr. BANG and joins Sun-cheol in marriage.

It's Not Her Sin (1959)

Yeong-suk is the foster sister of Seong-hui, a woman who is unable to bear children. When Yeong-suk's good-for-nothing boyfriend gets her pregnant, she has the baby and Seong-hui raises it as her own child while her husband is overseas working. Later, there is an incident that leads Yeong-suk to spend more time at Seong-hui's house. She develops maternal feelings and decides that she wants the child back. Ultimately, Yeong-suk plans to tell the whole truth to Seong-hui's husband, and Seong-hui fires a gun at her. Later, Yeong-suk leaves the child behind and goes off with another fiancé.

Chun-hui (1959)

A man loves a woman who works at a bar, but they run up against his father's opposition. One day the father goes to find her and implores her, saying that if she really loves the man she will end the relationship. She makes up her mind to end the relationship for the man she loves, and she refuses to see him again. Watching the disappointment man's figure receding in the distance, she dies a lonely death from the tuberculosis she has been suffering from.

Romance Papa (1960)

An insurance company employee whose children call him "Romance Papa" (KIM Seung-ho) lives in a happy home with his wife (JU Jeung-nyeo) and five children. The oldest daughter, Eum-jeon (CHOI Eun-hee), graduates from university and marries JEON Woo-taek (KIM Jin-gyu), a man who works at a meteorological observatory. The oldest son, Eo-jin (NAMGUNG Won), lies to his parents that he is attending college and works at a film set in order to become a film director. The

second daughter, Gop-dan (DO Geum-bong), is in college, and the second son Bareun-i (SHIN Sung-il) and the youngest daughter Ippeun-i (EOM Aeng-ran) are high school students. It is difficult stretching the father's paycheck for such a large family, but he is an optimist who shelters his family with smiles. But there is a wave of layoffs in the insurance company, and the father, a reliable employee, loses his job because of his advanced age. He does not tell his family for fear that they will despair. The son and daughters find out, but pretend not to know, and they look for a way to comfort their father. On his birthday, the whole gathers to share a happy time together.

Madam White Snake (1960)

Madam White Snake (CHOI Eun-hee), a thousand-year-old snake that has turned into a human, falls in love with the young pharmacist HEO Seon (SHIN Sung-il) and marries him. The two of them face a few crises, but their love for each other

does not bend. But the priest Beophae and the Goddess of Mercy tell the white snake, who has been reborn without permission, that she must return to the spirit world by the seventh of July. Sadly preparing to say her goodbyes, Madam White Snake falls victim to a plot by Dae-yun (CHOE Sam), the man who covets her, and is unable to carry out her promise. She risks her life for the husband she loves. Moved by their love, the Goddess of Mercy finally decides to allow their love.

To the Last Day (1960)

Captain KIM (KIM Jin-gyu) suffers a spine injury in the Korean War and is paralyzed from the waist down. His wife Hye-gyeong (CHOI Eun-hee) devotedly nurses her husband. While her family is fleeing to Daegu, the second daughter is killed. At the refugee camp, Captain KIM is once again admitted into the hospital, and Hye-gyeong is running a street stall when she meets Mr. JO (NAMGUNG Won). Orphaned in the war, Mr. JO asks Hye-gyeong to be his big sister, and the two of them quickly grow closer. One day, the husband visits the home and sees Hye-gyeong and Mr. JO walking together. He gets angry and returns to his hospital room. But when he meets his wife there, he pleads with her not to leave him, saying he cannot live without her. Hye-gyeong ends her relationship with Mr. JO and goes up to Seoul with her family. The couple establishes a center for war widows with nowhere to go and their children. They dream of a new hope, but when Seon-gyeong dies in a traffic accident they are thrust once again into despair. Hye-gyeong lies in bed without eating or drinking.

Just as the widows are about to leave the center, she gathers herself and goes out to build up their courage.

SEONG Chun-hyang (1961)

Chun-hyang, the daughter of a *gisaeng*, loves Master LEE, the son of an aristocratic family, but they are forced apart, and when she refuses a village magistrate's order to become his mistress, she is thrown in prison. LEE passes the state examination, returns to the village and rescues Chun-hyang. Based on a traditional Korean novel.

Prince Yeonsan (1961)

Telling the tumultuous chronicle of Prince Yeonsan, this is a leading historical piece of the early 1960s. Yeonsan (SHIN Yeong-gyun), the son of Seongjong (KIM Dong-won) is shocked one day to discover that he is the son of the deposed Queen YUN (JU Jeung-nyeo). After acceding to the throne, he tries to reinstate his mother's status, but runs into the opposition of the retainers, including Queen Mother In-su (JEON Ok). His personality rapidly becomes twisted. He becomes extremely coarse and lapses into drink and debauchery, carrying out horrible deeds. After seeing the image of his mother being unjustly executed in Dreams, his feelings become even more chaotic. Learning of his mother's unjust situation from his grandmother (HAN Eun-jin) and receiving a jacket stained with her blood, Yeonsan carries out his blood vengeance on all people involved with the deposed queen.

My Mother and Her Guest (1961)

Her grandmother (HAN Eun-jin), mother (CHOI Eun-hee) and maid (DO Geum-bong) are all "widows," so little Ok-hee's (JEON Yeong-seon) house is referred to as the "widows' house." Mr. HAN (KIM Jin-gyu), a friend of her uncle, comes into the house as a boarder. Six-year-old Ok-hee, who has never seen her father, follows HAN as if he were her father. Her mother and HAN secretly develop feelings for each other, and Ok-hee goes back and forth between the two playing the part of go-between. Through Ok-hee, HAN sends a letter confessing his love for her mother. But she is worried about her mother-in-law and daughter and rejects HAN's love. He leaves for Seoul.

Evergreen Tree (1961)

A man and woman from a specialized school each go down to the country with the intention of educating the agricultural villages. He sets up a village hall and leads the village youths, while she establishes a school and works to eradicate illiteracy. But the effects of vicious suppression by the Japanese

come upon them, and he is captured by the police, while she collapses from overwork. The day he is released, she sadly dies without ever realizing her passion for the village. Based on SHIM Hoon's novel *Sangnoksu.*

Yeonsan the Tyrant (1962)

The immoral acts of Prince Yeonsan and JANG Nok-su (DO Geum-bong) grow ever more outrageous with each passing year. PARK Won-jong (KIM Jin-gyu), who has lost his older sister and father to Yeonsan's barbaric acts, finally prepares a coup d'état. On the day it is to take place, Yeonsan slays JANG Nok-su and repents his past deeds, but with the coup he is deposed and sent into exile. Based on PARK Jonghwa's *Geumsam-ui Pi (Blood on a Gold Jacket).*

The Red Gate (1962)

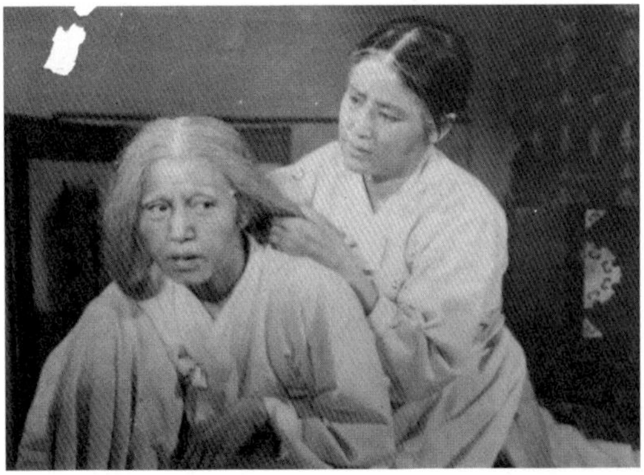

The daughter-in-law (CHOI Eun-hee) of an upper-class home tries to maintain her chastity as a young widow, but then falls into a romance with a farmhand (SHIN Yeong-gyun), which transcends class boundaries. One rainy day, the two of them make love in a mill, and she becomes pregnant and gives birth, but the farmhand is chased away holding the bloody newborn in his arms. Much later, the grown son goes to find his mother, but she is unable to even speak his name and sends him back. Her feelings come from the moral value that a widow must remain chaste. The grandmother (HAN Eun-jin) cannot bear to watch this, and calls to the son as he leaves, then collapses.

A Reluctant Prince (1963)

The late Joseon Era, when secret feuds between political parties were intense. Upon the death of Heonjong, the king's grandson Won-beom (SHIN Yeong-gyun), who is living as a common bachelor on Ganghwa Island, rises to the throne as King Cheoljong overnight. The story deals with a woman that Cheoljeong met on Ganghwa Island.

King Cheoljong and Bongnyeo (1963)

Cheoljong has become king, but he cannot forget Bongnyeo, the woman whose company he enjoyed on Ganghwa Island, and when the queen learns of this she summons Bongnyeo for a reunion with Cheoljong. Bongnyeo advises the king to be a virtuous leader respected by all the people, and Cheoljong, inspired by this, devotes himself to governing. But he ends up deposed after a short time, unable to realize his wish, due to the scheming of the faction of Queen Mother CHO.

Rice (1963)

Disabled former soldier CHA Yong (SHIN Yeong-gyun) learns that his father is seriously ill and returns home to the Muju Gucheon-dong gorge. After the father dies, Yong becomes firmly convinced that he will escape from poverty and establishes a plan to bore a tunnel through the rocky mountain and deliver water to the barren land. Gathering the people of the village, he goes to the village government and requests funding, but the public officials delay giving their support, using the election as an excuse. The villagers work together to build the tunnel, but one by one they drop out from malnutrition and overwork, leading Yong to become doubtful. Also, the village's wealthiest man, Assemblyman SONG (CHOE Sam), dislikes Yong and begins to create obstacles for the project. SONG's daughter, Jung-hee (CHOI Eun-hee), is engaged to marry Yong, but he declines to meet her after injuring his leg. Within this situation, Yong overcomes various harsh realities and succeeds at his engineering project.

Romance Gray (1963)

A middle-aged professor (KIM Seung-ho) who has been a faithful family man and chairman KIM of the Daeyeong company (KIM Hui-gap) each meet young bar girls, Man-ja (CHOI Eun-hee) and Bo-yeong (CHO Mi-ryeong) respectively, setting them up as mistresses and going back and forth between their two residences, trying to assuage the sadness of lives that are slowly entering their twilight. Learning about this, their wives (HAN Eun-jin and HWANG Jeong-sun) have a meeting to come up with a plan at the "Honeybee Club," a gathering for wives. They band up and barge into the mistresses' homes. Man-ja and Bo-yeong, the other women for Romance Gray, defend themselves to the wives by saying that they too are victims and that even mistresses have rights, but out of guilt for ruining the homes of others, they decide to bow out for the happiness of the married couples, and the two of them board a train for Busan. The men reflect over

their brief foray astray and the wives make them look once again at how they are now. Both homes are reborn as more harmonious environments.

Red Muffler (1964)

In 1952, at the height of the Korean War, new pilots move into the Air Force Gangreung area, including First Lieutenant BAE Dae-bong (CHOE Mu-ryong). The trainees grow into pilots under the instruction of Major NA Gwan-jung (SHIN Yeong-gyun), whose nickname is "Wild

Boar." One day, Lt. BAE is introduced by NA to Ji-seon (CHOI Eun-hee), the widow of one of NA's colleagues, NO Do-sun (NAMGUNG Won), and he falls in love with her. NA, who has been taking care of Ji-seon after her husband's death, sincerely congratulates Ji-seon and BAE on their new love. Shortly after their marriage, the pilots head out to carry out a mission that even the US forces could not succeed at. In their operation, BAE encounters a situation just like the one in which NO died, but he is rescued in the nick of time. But NA is killed after carrying out the operation successfully.

Deaf Samryong-i (1964)

Samryong (KIM Jin-gyu) is a kind and virtuous deaf farmhand. He cannot forget the kindness of Mr. OH, who took him in when he had nowhere to go, and he serves his master's home with all his heart. One day, Sun-deok (CHOI Eun-hee) comes into the home, sold to the master's brutish son Gwang-sik (PARK No-sik). With his own attentions on the maid Chu-wol (DO Geum-bong), he beats Sun-deok severely. Samryong feels pity for Sun-deok, crying her time away because of her husband, and he secretly pines for her. Meanwhile, he spreads a rumor about Gwang-sik and Chu-wol's affair and ends up beaten to within an inch of his life for it. On the night that Samryong is chased away, an unexplained fire breaks out in Mr. OH's home. Samryong rescues Sun-deok and even Gwang-sik, but does not emerge from the house himself.

The Mountain (1967)

Year 1959. LEE Il-seok (SHIN Yeong-gyun), who is obsessed with coal-mining development, picks up a check dropped by tea-room madam YUN Jung-ok (CHOI Eun-hee) and returns it to her. Coming to like him, Jung-ok learns that he is going around trying to find funding for coal development, but with nothing to show for

it, and she makes up her mind to help him. She sells the tea room, supplies the funding and goes to work in a *gisaeng* house. Unable to forget Il-seok, she awaits his letters, but there is no news for the next year. She cannot bear waiting any longer and goes to a mountain village in Gangwon Province to find him. One day, she discovers coal, and gets money by offering herself to Director KIM for the night. With that money, Il-seok succeeds in producing coal of the highest quality from the mine. But then the roughs who dug the mountain come to Il-seok and threaten him, and they end up telling him how Jung-ok came up with the funding. Furious, he denounces her and intends to tear down the coal mine. The roughs hatch a plan to take advantage of the opportunity and kill Il-seok. He ends up buried in the mine due to their plan. He is pulled out, but he does not survive, dying in Jung-ok's arms.

Mounted Bandits (1967)

An activist for Korean independence who works in Manchuria is visited one day by a Japanese military police captain who tells him that he will release Korean independence fighters imprisoned by the Japanese military police if the activist will rescue the English consul's daughter, who has been kidnapped by bandits. He accepts and rescues the daughter, but the regiment does not carry out its promise. The activists ambush a Japanese military train and has a grisly battle with the Japanese army, ultimately rescuing the Korean independence fighters being transported on the train.

Traces (1967)

Japanese artist Noguchi (OH Yeong-il), a teacher at a Korean school for girls, rescues PARK Dong-ho (LEE Dae-yeop), a Korean independence fighter who is being pursued by the Japanese police. To repay him for this, PARK promises to show Noguchi a traditional dance from the Joseon era and introduces him to KIM Yeong-sun (MUN Hui), an initiate in traditional dance. Deeply moved after seeing Yeong-sun's performance, Noguchi falls in love with her and wishes to paint a picture of her dancing. Yeong-sun, who has lost her parents to the Japanese army, loathes the Japanese, but finds herself falling in love with Noguchi despite herself. Visiting his house to gain approval of the marriage, Yeong-sun discovers that Noguchi's father is the very soldier who killed her father at the time of the March 1 independence movement and runs from the house. Their romance finished, Noguchi completes his painting, which is exhibited by the government under the title "Traces of the Joseon dynasty." Noguchi learns the reason for Yeong-sun's departure from Dong-ho. Making up his mind to ask her forgiveness, Noguchi decides to flee on a train. Dong-ho, who sees no reason to fight for the Japanese, also joins Noguchi in his escape, but on the way to Seoul he is injured and dies. After the liberation of Korea, Noguchi's father is killed by Korean youths. Noguchi visits Yeong-sun, but she treats him coldly, and he ends up committing suicide.

Eunuch (1968)

Ja-ok (YUN Jeong-hui), the high-born daughter of *champan* KIM (CHOE Nam-hyeon), and Jeong-ho (SHIN Sung-il), the son of a low-ranking official, have grown up in the same village and love one another. But KIM has a fierce ambition to increase his power, and when he learns of their relationship, he turns Jeong-ho into a eunuch and sends Ja-ok into the Royal Court as a court lady, intending to increase the family power by turning her into a royal concubine. Ja-ok and Jeong-ho still love each other and meet secretly in the palace, but they are found out. The king deliberately takes Ja-ok to bed, but when she behaves in an insolent manner there, she is shut off in a second palace. Meanwhile, the master eunuch (PARK No-sik) sees the two lovers maintaining their true love in spite of Jeong-ho's castration and is reminded of his own trauma. Moved, he frees them. They flee into the mountains, but Jeong-ho is killed and Ja-ok is brought back to the Royal Court. *Champan* KIM's rank increases because of Ja-ok's pregnancy with the king's child, and the king favors her. But when the two are in bed, she stabs him in the neck with a gimlet that she has hidden in her mouth, then takes her own life.

Homeless (1968)

JANG (SHIN Yeong-gyun) was once a famed mounted bandit, but he is now homeless. One day, he is captured by some members of a guerrilla unit. Their leader, noting JANG's strength, asks him to get rid of Sam-man (CHOE Seong-ho), who is not paying his taxes. He has tried to collect excessive taxes because his position as leader was bought with money. In the fight between Sam-man and the guerrillas, Sam-man is killed, and they take his wife and child home in accordance with his final wishes. But she is not welcomed by her family. Chased away, the mother and child ask JANG to accompany them to the city so that she can find work. While there, he happens to meet YANG, who was a junior of his when he was a bandit in the past. Due to this meeting, he ends up getting mixed up in various incidents. When JANG returns a year later, she is being wooed by the rich and presentable Mr. SA. Secretly watching them, JANG is pained, but he leaves so that they can be happy.

A Woman's Life (1968)

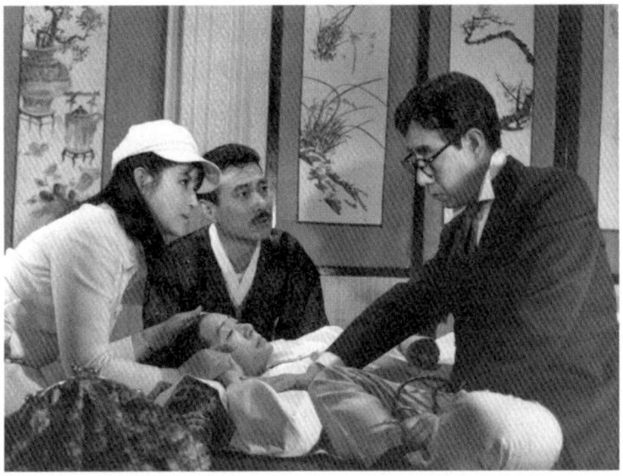

Nan-ju (CHOI Eun-hee) from the family of Master HAN of Chungju (KIM Dong-won), is visited by CHOI Jong-su (NAMGUNG Won), who says that he was schoolmate of her dead brother Tae-jun, and the two of them fall in love. Upon being taken into the family as a son-in-law, Jong-su reveals his true colors: he does not work, starts conflicts with the servants, and expresses disappointment that his wife's assets are fewer than he thought. One day, a servant girl, Bun-i, becomes pregnant, and when Nan-ju learns that the two of them have been in a relationship since before their engagement, she is shocked and faints. Bun-i is chased out of the house. Later, Jong-su begins an adulterous relationship with the wife of a close friend who is director of a local agency, and when the director learns of this, he is enraged and shoots Jong-su dead with a hunting rifle. Years later, Nan-ju's son Myeong-woon travels to Seoul to attend university. He gets into trouble at every turn, causing an accident while speeding with friends in his car, living in sin with Hee-sook (NAM Jeong-im) and getting sucked into gambling on mahjong. Rebelling against Nan-ju, he gives him only the role of paying money and cleaning up after him. Myeong-woon says that it was because of the "bad blood" of his father, shot dead after sleeping with another man's wife, and resents his mother. One day, Master HAN dies, and as the family fortunes gradually begin to decline, they are forced to sell the house in Chungju. Around this time, Bun-i, the servant girl chased away long ago, visits Nan-ju. She tells Nan-ju that she is living well in a wealthy home with her husband and three brothers and sisters. Later, still more misfortunes come upon Nan-ju's house, and she and Bun-i resignedly accept it as a woman's lot.

Women of the Joseon Dynasty (1969)

An omnibus film in three parts. Part One: "A Woman Must Obey Her Husband." So-yeon (NAM Jeong-im), daughter of Master GANG (PARK Am), is married to the dead Man-deuk, the son of Master AHN. Due to her marriage with the late son, So-yeon rises in stature as a chaste widow, and GANG's rank increases. She is praised for her chastity, but she is tired of living as a widow, and secretly makes up her mind to leave home. Learning of this, her father lies in wait and kills her with an arrow, making it look like she took her own life to follow her husband. After this, a gate is erected in praise of her chastity. Part Two: "The Seven Grounds for Divorce." Mrs. HAN (CHOI Eun-hee), unable to produce a male child in ten years of marriage, makes a fervent prayer, and on her way back meets Sung-chil (SHIN Yeong-gyun), a stuttering farmhand. She has an affair with him, becoming pregnant and ultimately having a son. Mrs. HAN's husband (NAMGUNG Won) goes to a doctor of Chinese medicine to get a prescription and learns that he is infertile. He demands that his wife tell him who the father of the child is. Faced with this crisis, she takes her life, leaving behind a message that he have faith in her. Part Three: "A Court Lady Must Live Only for the King." Bedchamber court lady LEE (KIM Ji-mi) has the task of watching the bed of the king every night. Watching the king with his concubine, she is unable to control her lust and runs outside. A military officer appears. He rapes LEE and she becomes pregnant. Under the protection of the ladies of the court, LEE has her child in the

Yeongodang, a secluded place within the Royal Court. In order to get her and her child out of the palace, they switch her for the body of another dead lady of the court. Ladies of the court can only leave the palace dead. As soon as the coffin containing the mother and child leaves the palace, a eunuch who has heard a rumor runs the coffin through with a spear, saying that he must check the body. He hears the cry of a child, but he senses what the court ladies are feeling and plays dumb. LEE safely escapes the palace.

The Snake Woman (1969)

A thousand-year-old white snake receives orders from the Devil and transforms into a beautiful woman who seduces the young scholar Seong-do, ultimately living with him and bearing his son. The snake then reveals her identity according to the Devil's order and tries to kill Seong-do, but she cannot bring herself to do it. The Devil turns her to stone, but through the benevolence of the Goddess of Mercy, she is brought back again as a human and lives happily ever after with Seong-do and their child.

A Thousand Year Old Fox (1969)

KIM Won-rang (SHIN Yeong-gyun) returns after driving away a band of thieves and attends a congratulatory feast offered by Queen Jin-seong (KIM Hye-jeong). That night, the queen seduces KIM, whom she has longed for since before ascending to the throne, and she orders KIM's wife Yeo-hwa (KIM Ji-su) driven out of the capital. Traveling through the forest with her child, Yeo-hwa meets mountain bandits who kill the child and try to rape Yeo-hwa. The fleeing Yeo-hwa dives into a pond. Belatedly learning of this, KIM comes running and fishes Yeo-hwa out of the pond, but there is a surprising warmth lingering in Yeo-hwa's body. Late at night, she awakens and, as though possessed, leaves the house, finds the bandits who killed her child and seduces and kills them. The thousand-year-old fox, who can only ascend to heaven after capturing and eating one thousand people, saved Yeo-hwa's life, and in exchange he borrows her body to exact his vengeance. Yeo-hwa sneaks into the dwelling of Queen Jin-seong and tries to kill her. Realizing that she is the fox, the queen intends to set fire to the temple where Yeo-hwa is staying. After the cock cries in the morning, Yeo-hwa is stabbed to death by KIM, who is taken away. After he is freed, he spurns the advances of Jin-seong, who has been chased from the throne, and watches over the grave of Yeo-hwa through snow and rain. He sits and turns into a skeleton.

Ghosts of Joseon (1970)

Prince Yeon-san attempts to violate Ya-hwa, the wife of the executed YUN Pil-woo. She follows her husband and commits suicide, leaving a final wish to her beloved cat to get revenge. Subsequently, the bodies of court women and patrolmen are found every morning in the palace, and the ghosts of YUN Pil-woo and Ya-hwa appear along with the sounds of a cat crying. YUN's friend, a royal guard named KIM Chung-won, is aided by the power of the high priest and chases away the spirits for the sake of the royal family.

The Evening Bell (1970)

The child of deaf parents grows up and gets a job. He has a girlfriend, but the director of the company he works at tries to get him to take care of his deaf daughter. However, she too has a deaf lover. One day, the son's girlfriend learns of this and disappears, wishing him happiness. The son persuades the director's daughter to marry her lover. The girlfriend finally returns from hiding.

Lady of the Court (1972)

The time is the Joseon dynasty. King Myeongjong dies, leaving behind his son as heir. His three concubines are driven out of the palace. One of them is named Bongnyeo. When she came to the palace as Myeongjong's lady-in-waiting in order to escape from poverty, she was already a week pregnant. After the king dies, the queen mother does not like the new king, so she brings Bongnyeo's young child into the position of crown prince in order to maintain her own power. When Bongnyeo returns to the palace, she confesses the truth to the queen mother's servants and confidants. She ends up facing danger because of the retainers' plotting. Byeong-cheol, Bongnyeo's husband and the father of the child, rescues them from the retainers.

The Three-Day Reign (1973)

November 1884, Late Joseon. In the Royal Palace, conservative forces depending on China and reformist forces depending on Japan are waging a fierce battle over royal authority. KIM Ok-gyun, a reformist, advises the king to eliminate the Chinese influence and proclaim independence, a proposal that the king gladly accepts. KIM's forces then take advantage of the anniversary of the founding of the postal service and effectively seize political power. But conservative spies secretly inform the Chinese of this, and the Chinese Yuan Shikai leads an army into Korea, reducing KIM's dream of independence to nothing after three days.

Woman with Half a Soul (1973)

Young Master HAN has to take 1,000 gold coins and go to the house of Yeon-hwa, but his money is stolen by mountain bandits, and he ends up staying at the home of Jang-soe, his old servant. The spirit of Yeon-hwa, who died after being unable to see her husband HAN, appears to him every night and shares the love that she could not give in this lifetime. Jang-soe sees his master associating with the ghost and calls a shaman, who performs an exorcism and applies an amulet, but without any effect. Finally, HAN comes to his senses and avoids the ghost of Yeon-hwa, but after he accedes to her request to make love one last time as man and wife, she breaks free from the curse of being a ghost and prepares to move on to the afterlife.

The Rose and the Wild Dog (1975)

Jun does not fit in as a worker at a rose garden outside of Hong Kong. He loads his truck with flowers and leaves. At a dock, he gives a bouquet of roses to a woman named Haeng-ja. She is rescued by Jun just as she is about to kill herself. Haeng-ja

gradually begins to feel affection for the cold Jun. Meanwhile, the Japanese Daehwajeon, who is chasing after the traitorous Jun, sends an old friend of Jun's named Sam-bin to Hong Kong. Haeng-ja follows Jun, who is now a wanted man, but ultimately the two of them are captures. However, just as they are in imminent danger, Sam-bin experiences a change of heart and rescues them. There is a gun battle between Sam-bin and Daehwajeon's gang, and Jun and Haeng-ja take advantage of this to board a boat, but both are killed by bullets fired by Daehwajeon's underlings.

Prisoner 407 (1976)

SEO Gang-hee, prisoner 407, recalls her life. She loved Ha-ryun despite her parents' objection. He was a Japanese detective who tricked her and hatched a plot to root out the independence fighters. As a result, Gang-hee went to prison, while Ha-ryun got a promotion and became engaged to the daughter of a Kwantung Army officer. One day, during a thunderstorm, Gang-hee escapes the prison with other prisoners and shows up at the hall where Ha-ryun's wedding is taking place. Nam-ju and Gang-hee fire a hail of bullets at Ha-ryun, and Nam-ju sacrifices her life for Gang-hee, grabbing the warden and falling from a railing.

Mayumi (1990)

KIM Seung-il and KIM Hyun-hee plan to blow up Korean Air Flight 858 from Baghdad to Seoul on November 28. They arrive in Belgrade with Japanese passports and get a hold of the bomb. Placing a blue shopping bag holding the radio detonator and liquid explosive on a shelf, they get off at a layover in Abu Dhabi. They attempt to leave with a transit visa, but are turned down, so without any other option they leave for Bahrain. Meanwhile, Flight 858 explodes over the Sea of Andaman, and the Korean government discovers the names "Shinichi" and "Mayumi" on the passenger manifest. As the terrorists go through the departure procedures to go to Rome, their passports are discovered to be fake and they are placed under guard, at which point they bite down on previously prepared suicide pellets. Shinichi dies immediately, but Mayumi gets emergency treatment and is

brought to the Korean investigators. There is a trial over the bombing, and it is only when she sees the grieving family members at the trial that Mayumi realizes what she has done. She cries out for them to kill her so that she can atone for her sins.

Vanished (1994)

Late one night, a large cargo plane arrives at an international airport carrying a tightly sealed container as a diplomatic pouch. Inside is PARK Jin-wook, a former Minister of National Security kidnapped in the United States for crimes against the state and the writing of memoirs as a scapegoat for a competition of loyalty. The current Minister of National Security, LEE Sang-gyu, takes this information disinterestedly, then reports the success of the kidnapping operation to President HAN Sung-tae. The president directs LEE to get PARK on their side within 48 hours. Meanwhile, in a southern port city, large-scale demonstrations with protestors crying "Down with the dictatorship" are taking place, and things progress to an unpredictable state of uneasiness as the government invokes the Garrison Act, mobilizing the military and tanks. LEE asks PARK, who has been taken a special cell, to stop the writing of his memoirs, but PARK stubbornly refuses, saying that he has no choice but to write his memoirs with the intent of fully realizing and repenting for the corrupt history of the past 18 years. In the cell, painted totally white, Jin-wook looks back quietly at the vortex of the history of 18 years before.

A Winter Story (unreleased) (2004)

Drama about the conflicts between a senile father-in-law and daughter-in-law and how they overcome them.

Filmography

* Where two English titles are given, the second is the title provided by the Korean Film Archive's KMDB.

** Questions about these films' importation and exhibition can be directed to the Korean Film Archive.

FILMOGRAPHY

The Evil Night (Agya)

1952 (Film no longer extant)
Production Company: Cinema Art Association
Script: LEE Gwang-rae
Cinematography: LEE Seong-hwi
Editing: SHIN Sang-ok
Music: JO Baek-bong
Lighting: Unknown
Starring: HWANG Nam, LEE Min-ja, KIM Woong, MUN Jeong-suk, CHOI Eun-hee
No film storage information

Korea

1954 (Film no longer extant)
Production Company: Cinema Art Association
Script: YU Du-yeon
Cinematography: BYEON In-jip
Lighting: KIM Seong-chun
Editing: SHIN Sang-ok
Music: JO Baek-bong
Starring: CHOI Eun-hee, KIM Dong-won, YUN In-ja, LEE Hae-rang
No film storage information

Dream (Kkum)

1955 (Film no longer extant)
Production Company: Seorabeol Film Corporation
Script: SHIN Sang-ok
Cinematography: PARK Hui-yeong
Lighting: CHOE Jin
Editing: SHIN Sang-ok
Music: KIM Seong-tae
Starring: HWANG Nam, CHOI Eun-hee, JANG Il, CHOE Yong, YANG Woon, GO Seol-bong
No film storage information

The Youth (Jeolmeun Geudeul)

1955 / 35mm / 89 min / B&W
Production Company: Seoul Film Company
Script: LEE Hyeong-pyo
Cinematography: YANG Bo-hwan
Lighting: YUN Yeong-eun
Editing: KIM Deok-jin
Music: KIM Dong-jin

Starring: CHOI Eun-hee, CHOE Mu-ryong, GANG Gye-sik, CHOE Nam-hyeon, JANG Il, MUN Jeong-suk
Print stored at Korean Film Archive

Pagoda of No Shadows/The Shadowless Pagoda (Muyeongtap)

1957 / 35mm / 117 min / 1.33:1 / B&W
Production Company: Seoul Film Company/Shin Sang-ok Productions
Script: LEE Hyeong-pyo
Cinematography: SEO Yeon-hwi, CHOE Gyeong-ok
Lighting: KIM Seong-chun
Editing: KIM Yeong-hui
Music: NA Un-yeong
Starring: CHOI Eun-hee, HAN Eun-jin, GWAK Geon, KIM Seung-ho
Print stored at Korean Film Archive

A College Woman's Confession (Eoneu Yeodaesaeng-ui Gobaek)

1958 / 35mm / 100 min / 1.33:1 / B&W
Production Company: Seoul Film Company, Shin Sang-ok Productions
Script: SHIN Sang-ok, JO Nam-sa
Cinematography: GANG Beom-gu
Lighting: LEE Han-chan
Editing: KIM Yeong-hui
Music: KIM Yong-hwan
Starring: CHOI Eun-hee, KIM Seung-ho, YU Gye-seon, CHOE Hyeon
Print stored at Korean Film Archive

A Flower in Hell/A Flower in Hell (Jiokhwa)

1958 / 35mm / 86 min / 1.33:1 / B&W
Production Company: Seoul Film Company
Script: LEE Jeong-seon
Cinematography: GANG Beom-gu
Lighting: LEE Gyu-chang
Editing: KIM Yeong-hui
Music: SON Mok-in
Starring: CHOI Eun-hee, KIM Hak, JO Hae-won, GANG Seon-hui
Print stored at Korean Film Archive

Dongsimcho

1959 / 35mm / 125 min / 1.33:1 / B&W
Production Company: Korea Film Distribution Company
Script: LEE Bong-rae, JO Nam-sa
Cinematography: LEE Hyeong-pyo
Lighting: LEE Gye-chang
Editing: KIM Yeong-hui
Music: KIM Seong-hui
Starring: CHOI Eun-hee, KIM Jin-gyu, EOM Aeng-ran, JU Jeung-nyeo
Print stored at Korean Film Archive

Lee Seungman and the Independence Movement/Independence Association and Young Lee Shung-man (Dongnip Hyeophoe-wa Cheongnyeon LEE Seung-man)

1959 / 35mm / 133 min / 1.33:1 / B&W
Production Company: Korea Entertainment Inc.
Script: LIM Hui-jae, LEE Jeong-seon

Cinematography: LIM Byeong-ho, BAE Seong-hak
Lighting: GO Hae-jin, KIM Seong-chun
Editing: YANG Ju-nam
Music: KIM Dae-hyeon, YUN Yong-ha
Starring: KIM Jin-gyu, KIM Seung-ho, HWANG Jeong-sun, CHOE Nam-hyeon
Print stored at Korean Film Archive

A A Sister's Garden (Jamae-ui Hwawon)

1959 / 35mm / 119 min / 1.33:1 / B&W
Production Company: Seoul Film Company
Script: JO Nam-sa
Cinematography: CHOE Gyeong-ok
Lighting: LEE Gyu-chang
Editing: SHIN Sang-ok
Starring: CHOI Eun-hee, CHOE Ji-hui, NAMGUNG Won, KIM Seok-hun, KIM Seung-ho, JU Seon-tae, CHOE Nam-hyeon, HAN Eun-jin, AHN Sung-ki
Print stored at Korean Film Archive

It's Not Her Sin (Geu Yeoja-ui Joe-ga Anida)

1959 / 35mm / 104 min / 1.33:1 / B&W
Production Company: Seoul Film Company
Script: SHIN Sang-ok
Cinematography: CHOE Gyeong-ok, JEONG Hae-jun
Lighting: LEE Han-chan, SON Yeong-cheol
Editing: KIM Yeong-hui
Music: KIM Yong-hwan
Starring: NO Neung-geol, CHOI Eun-hee, JU Jeung-nyeo, LEE Min, JEON Taek-i
Print stored at Korean Film Archive

Chun-hie

1959 (Film no longer extant)
Production Company: Hyundai Film Company
Script: KIM Gang-yun
Cinematography: SHIN Sang-ok
Lighting: LEE Han-chan
Editing: SHIN Sang-ok
Starring: KIM Seok-hun, CHOI Eun-hee, JEON Taek-i, GO Seon-ae, KIM Seung-ho

Romance Papa/A Romantic Papa

1960 / 35mm / 131 min / 1.33:1 / B&W
Production Company: Shin Films
Script: KIM Hui-chang
Cinematography: JEONG Hae-jun
Lighting: LEE Gye-chang
Editing: KIM Yeong-hui
Music: KIM Seong-dae
Starring: KIM Seung-ho, JU Jeung-nyeo, CHOI Eun-hee, KIM Jin-gyu, NAMGUNG Won, SHIN Sung-il, DO Geum-bong, EOM Aeng-ran
Print stored at Korean Film Archive

Madam White Snake (Baeksa Buin)

1960 / 35mm / 100 min / 1.33:1 / B&W
Production Company: Shin Films
Script: LIM Hui-jae
Cinematography: CHOE Gyeong-ok, JEONG Hae-jun
Lighting: LEE Gye-chang
Editing: KIM Yeong-hui
Music: JEONG Yun-ju

Starring: CHOI Eun-hee, SHIN Sung-il, HAN Eun-jin, CHOE Sam
Print stored at Korean Film Archive

To the Last Day (I LIfe Tahadorok)

1960 / 35mm / 109 min / 1.33:1 / B&W
Production Company: Shin Films
Script: LIM Hui-jae, LEE Hyeong-pyo
Cinematography: JEONG Hae-jun
Lighting: LEE Gye-chang
Editing: KIM Yeong-hui
Music: KIM Seong-tae
Starring: CHOI Eun-hee, KIM Jin-gyu, NAMGUNG Won, SHIN Sung-il
Print stored at Korean Film Archive

SEONG Chun-hyang

1961 / 35mm / 107 min / 2.35:1 / Color
Production Company: Shin Films
Script: LIM Hui-jae
Cinematography: LEE Hyeong-pyo
Lighting: LEE Gye-chang
Editing: KIM Yeong-hui
Music: JEONG Yun-ju
Starring: CHOI Eun-hee, KIM Jin-gyu, DO Geum-bong, HEO Jang-gang
Print stored at Korean Film Archive

Prince Yeonsan/Prince Yeonsan

1961 / 35mm / 133 min / 2.35:1 / Color
Production Company: Shin Films
Script: LIM Hui-jae
Cinematography: BAE Seong-hak, JEONG Hae-jun
Lighting: LEE Gye-chang
Editing: KIM Yeong-hui
Music: JEONG Yun-ju
Starring: SHIN Yeong-gyun, KIM Jin-gyu, DO Geum-bong, SHIN Sung-il
Print stored at Korean Film Archive

My Mother and Her Guest/A Mother and a Guest (Sarangbang Sonnim-gwa Eomeoni)

1961 / 35mm / 102 min / 2.35:1 / B&W
Production Company: Shin Films
Script: LIM Hui-jae
Cinematography: CHOE Su-yeong
Lighting: LEE Gye-chang
Editing: YANG Seong-ran
Music: JEONG Yun-ju
Starring: CHOI Eun-hee, JEON Yeong-seon, KIM Jin-gyu, HAN Eun-jin
Print stored at Korean Film Archive

Evergreen Tree (Sangroksu)

1961 / 35mm / 110 min / 2.35:1 / B&W
Production Company: Shin Films
Script: KIM Gang-yun
Cinematography: BAE Seong-hak
Lighting: LEE Gyu-chang

Editing: KIM Yeong-hui
Music: JEONG Yun-ju
Starring: CHOI Eun-hee, SHIN Yeong-gyun, HEO Jang-gang, DO Geum-bong
Print stored at Korean Film Archive

Yeonsan the Tyrant/Tyrant Yeonsan (Pokgun Yeonsan)

1962 / 35mm / 192 min / 2.35:1 /Color
Production Company: Shin Films
Script: LIM Hui-jae
Cinematography: JEONG Hae-jun
Lighting: LEE Gyu-chang
Editing: KIM Yeong-hui
Music: JEONG Yun-ju
Starring: SHIN Yeong-gyun, DO Geum-bong, KIM Jin-gyu, LEE Ye-chun
Print stored at Korean Film Archive

The Red Gate/Bound by Chastity Rule (Yeolnyeomun)

1962 / 35mm / 100 min / 2.35:1 / B&W
Production Company: Shin Films
Script: KIM Gang-yun
Cinematography: JEONG Hae-jun
Lighting: LEE Gyu-chang
Editing: KIM Yeong-hui
Music: JEONG Yun-ju
Starring: CHOI Eun-hee, SHIN Yeong-gyun, KIM Dong-won, HAN Eun-jin
Print stored at Korean Film Archive

A Reluctant Prince/A Reluctance Prince (Ganghwadoryeong)

1963 / 35mm / 126 min / 2.35:1 / B&W
Production Company: Shin Films
Script: LIM Hui-jae
Cinematography: KIM Yeong-in
Lighting: LEE Gyu-chang
Editing: OH Seong-hwan
Music: JEONG Yun-ju
Starring: CHOI Eun-hee, SHIN Yeong-gyun, KIM Seung-ho, HWANG Jeong-sun
Print stored at Korean Film Archive

King Cheoljong and Bongnyeo/King Cheoljong and Bongnyeo (Cheoljong-gwa Bongnyeo)

1963 / 35mm / 100 min / B&W (original negative existing)
Production Company: Shin Films
Script: LEE Seo-gu
Cinematography: KIM Jong-rae
Lighting: MA Yong-cheon
Editing: KIM Yeong-hui
Music: JEONG Yun-ju
Starring: SHIN Yeong-gyun, CHOI Eun-hee, KIM Hui-gap, HAN Eun-jin
Print stored at Korean Film Archive

Rice (Ssal)

1963 / 35mm / 124 min / 2.35:1 / B&W
Production Company: Shin Films
Script: KIM Gang-yun
Cinematography: KIM Yeong-in

Lighting: LEE Gye-chang
Editing: YANG Seong-nan
Music: JEONG Yun-ju
Starring: SHIN Yeong-gyun, CHOI Eun-hee, NAMGUNG Won, CHOE Geol
Print stored at Korean Film Archive

The Torchlight (Hwaetbul)

1963 (Film no longer extant)
Running time and film specifics unknown
Production Company: Shin Films
Script: LIM Hui-jae
Cinematography: KIM Yong-in
Lighting: LEE Gyu-chang
Editing: OH Seong-hwan
Music: JEONG Yun-ju
Starring: SHIN Yeong-gyun, CHOI Eun-hee, LEE Ye-chun, HAN Eun-jin

Romance Gray/Love Affair

1963 / 35mm / 125 min / 1.33:1 / B&W
Production Company: Shin Films
Script: LIM Hui-jae
Cinematography: JEONG Hae-jun
Lighting: LEE Gyu-chang
Editing: KIM Yeong-hui
Music: JEONG Yun-ju
Starring: KIM Seung-ho, CHOI Eun-hee, SHIN Yeong-gyun, HAN Eun-jin
Print stored at Korean Film Archive

The Red Muffler (Ppalgan Mahura)

1964 / 35mm / 1.85:1 / Color
Production Company: Shin Films
Script: KIM Gang-yun
Cinematography: KIM Jong-rae, JEONG Hae-jun
Lighting: LEE Gyu-chang
Editing: YANG Seong-ran
Music: HWANG Mun-pyeong
Starring: CHOI Eun-hee, SHIN Yeong-gyun, CHOE Mu-ryong, HAN Eun-jin
Print stored at Korean Film Archive

Deaf Samryongi (Beongeori Samryong)

1964 / 35mm / 86 min / 2.35:1 / B&W
Production Company: Shin Films
Script: KIM Gang-yun
Cinematography: KIM Jong-rae
Lighting: MA Yong-cheon
Editing: OH Seong-hwan
Music: JEONG Yun-ju
Starring: KIM Jin-gyu, CHOI Eun-hee, PARK No-sik, DO Geum-bong
Print stored at Korean Film Archive

The Story of Bae, Local Official (Bae Bijang)

1965 (Film no longer extant)
Running time and film specifics unknown
Production Company: Shin Films
Script: KIM Gang-yun
Cinematography: JEONG Hae-jun

Lighting: JEONG Gyeong-hui
Editing: OH Seong-hwan
Music: JEONG Yun-ju
Starring: KIM Seung-ho, CHOI Eun-hee, KIM Hui-gap, CHOE Nam-hyeon

The Mountain (San)

1967 / 35mm / 91 min / 2.35:1 / B&W
Production Company: Shin Films
Script: CHOE Geum-dong
Cinematography: CHOE Seung-woo
Lighting: MA Yong-cheon
Editing: OH Seong-hwan
Music: JEONG Yun-ju
Starring: CHOI Eun-hee, SHIN Yeong-gyun, KIM Hui-gap, YANG Chun
Print stored at Korean Film Archive

Mounted Bandits (Majeok)

1967 (Film no longer extant)
Running time and film specifics unknown
Production Company: Deokheung Films
Script: GWAK Il-lo
Cinematography: CHOE Seung-woo
Lighting: KIM Dae-jin
Editing: OH Seong-hwan
Music: HWANG Mun-pyeong
Starring: SHIN Yeong-gyun, Baba Printong, PARK No-sik, CHOI Eun-hee

Dreams (Kkum)

1967 / 35mm / 91 min / 1.33:1 / Color
Production Company: Anyang Films
Script: OH Yeong-jin
Cinematography: CHOE Seung-woo, HONG Seok-jeong
Lighting: KIM Dae-jin
Editing: OH Seong-hwan
Music: JEONG Yun-ju
Starring: SHIN Yeong-gyun, KIM Hye-jeong, YANG Hun, BANG Su-il
Print stored at Korean Film Archive

Traces (Ijo Janyeong)

1967 / 35mm / 80 min / 2.35:1 / Color
Production Company: Shin Films
Script: SONG San-seon-sam
Cinematography: CHOE Seung-woo
Lighting: MA Yong-cheon
Editing: OH Seong-hwan
Music: JEONG Yun-ju
Starring: OH Yeong-il, MUN Hui, LEE Dae-yeop, LEE Sun-jae
Print stored at Korean Film Archive

Tender Heart (Dajeong Bulsim)

1967 / 35mm / 100 min / 2.35:1 / Color
Production Company: Shin Films
Script: CHOE Geum-dong
Cinematography: KIM Jong-rae
Lighting: KIM Dae-jin
Editing: OH Seong-hwan
Music: KIM Hui-jo

Starring: CHOI Eun-hee, KIM Jin-gyu, PARK No-sik, CHOE Seong-ho
Print stored at Korean Film Archive

Eunuch (Naesi)

1968 / 35mm / 90 min / 2.35:1 / Color
Production Company: Shin Films
Script: GWAK Il-lo
Cinematography: CHOE Seung-woo
Lighting: HAM Wan-seop
Editing: OH Seong-hwan
Music: JEONG Yun-ju
Starring: SHIN Sung-il, YUN Jeong-hui, PARK No-sik, NAMGUNG Won
Print stored at Korean Film Archive

Homeless/The Homeless Wanderer (Musukja)

1968 / 35mm / 97 min / 2.35:1 / Color
Production Company: Shin Films
Script: GWAK Il-lo
Cinematography: CHOE Seung-woo
Lighting: MA Yong-cheon
Editing: OH Seong-hwan
Music: HWANG Mun-pyeong
Starring: SHIN Yeong-gyun, CHOI Eun-hee, CHOE Seong-ho, KIM Jeong-hun
Print stored at Korean Film Archive

A Woman's Life/The Life of a Woman (Yeoja-ui Ilsaeng)

1968 / 35mm / 115 min / 2.35:1 / Color
Production Company: Shin Films
Script: JEON Beom-seong
Cinematography: CHOE Seung-woo
Lighting: HAM Wan-seop
Editing: OH Seong-hwan
Music: JEON Jeong-geun
Starring: CHOI Eun-hee, DO Geum-bong, NAM Jeong-im, NAMGUNG Won
Print stored at Korean Film Archive

Prince Daewon/Prince Daewon

1968 / 35mm / 120 min / 2.35:1 / Color
Production Company: Anyang Films
Script: LEE Sang-hyeon
Cinematography: CHOE Seung-woo
Lighting: KIM Dae-jin
Editing: OH Seong-hwan
Music: JEONG Yun-ju
Starring: SHIN Yeong-gyun, KIM Ji-mi, CHOE Nam-hyeon, HEO Jang-gang
Print stored at Korean Film Archive

Day Dream (Janghanmong)

1969 / 35mm / 100 min / 2.35:1 / Color
Production Company: Shin Films
Script: SHIN Sang-ok
Cinematography: CHOE Seung-woo
Lighting: MA Yong-cheon
Editing: OH Seong-hwan

Music: HWANG Mun-pyeong
Starring: SHIN Sung-il, YUN Jeong-hui, NAMGUNG Won, HAN Eun-jin
Print stored at Korean Film Archive

Private Kim (Yukgun Kim Ilbyeong)

1969 (Film no longer extant)
Running time and film specifics unknown
Production Company: Shin Films
Script: GWAK Il-lo
Cinematography: CHOE Seung-woo
Lighting: MA Yong-cheon
Editing: OH Seong-hwan
Music: HWANG Mun-pyeong
Starring: SHIN Yeong-gyun, CHOI Eun-hee, NAM Jeong-im, KIM Sang-guk

Women of the Joseon Dynasty/Women of Yi-Dynasty (Ijo Yeoin Janhoksa)

1969 / 35mm / 84 min / 2.35:1 / Color
Production Company: Shin Films
Script: LEE Sang-hyeon
Cinematography: CHOE Seung-woo
Lighting: MA Yong-cheon
Editing: OH Seong-hwan
Music: JEONG Yun-ju
Starring: CHOI Eun-hee, KIM Ji-mi, YUN Jeong-hui, NAM Jeong-im
Print stored at Korean Film Archive

Eunuch 2 (Naesi [Sok])

1969 (Film no longer extant)
Running time and film specifics unknown
Production Company: Shin Films
Script: GWAK Il-lo
Cinematography: CHOE Seung-woo
Lighting: MA Yong-cheon
Editing: OH Seong-hwan
Music: HWANG Mun-pyeong
Starring: SHIN Sung-il, MUN Hui, SHIN Yeong-gyun, DO Geum-bong, HWANG Hae

The Snake Woman/Dead Woman (Sanyeo)

1969 / 35mm / 100 min / 2.35:1 / Color
Production Company: Shin Films
Script: GWAK Il-lo
Cinematography: CHOE Seung-woo
Lighting: MA Yong-cheon
Editing: OH Seong-hwan
Music: JEON Jeong-geun
Starring: OH Yeong-il, KIM Hye-jeong, BAEK Il-seop, LEE Hyang
Print stored at Korean Film Archive

Women Above Men/Women Placed Above Men (Yeoseong Sangwi Sidae)

1969 / 35mm / 88 min / 2.35:1 / Color
Production Company: Shin Films
Script: GWAK Il-lo
Cinematography: CHOE Seung-woo
Lighting: MA Yong-cheon
Editing: OH Seong-hwan

Music: HWANG Mun-pyeong
Starring: NAM Jeong-im, NAMGUNG Won, PARK Am, HAN Eun-jin
Print stored at Korean Film Archive

A Thousand Year Old Fox/Thousand Years Old Fox (Cheonnyeonho)

1969 / 35mm / 89 min / 2.35:1 / Color
Production Company: Shin Films
Script: GWAK Il-lo
Cinematography: CHOE Seung-woo
Lighting: HAM Wan-seop
Editing: OH Seong-hwan
Music: JEONG Yun-ju
Starring: SHIN Yeong-gyun, KIM Ji-su, KIM Hye-jeong, GANG Gye-sik
Print stored at Korean Film Archive

Ghosts of Joseon/A Ghost Story of Joseon Dynasty (Ijo Goedam)

1970 / 35mm / 81 min / 2.35:1 / Color
Production Company: Shin-a Films
Script: GWAK Il-lo
Cinematography: CHOE Seung-woo
Editing: OH Seong-hwan
Music: JEONG Yun-ju
Starring: JO Su-hyeon, CHOE Ji-suk, JEON Yeong-ju, LEE Gang-hui
Print stored at Korean Film Archive

The Evening Bell (Manjong)

1970 / 35mm / 100 min / 2.35:1 / Color
Production Company: Shin Films
Script: LEE Hyeong-woo, LEE Hee-woo
Cinematography: CHOE Seung-woo
Lighting: MA Yong-cheon
Editing: OH Seong-hwan
Music: JEON Jeong-geun
Starring: CHOI Eun-hee, KIM Jin-gyu, SHIN Sung-il, KIM Chang-suk
Print stored at Korean Film Archive

Last Battle in Pyeongyang/The Last Flight to Pyongyang (Pyeongyang Pokgyeokdae)

1971 / Running time and film specifics unknown
Production Company: Anyang Films
Script: GWAK Il-lo
Starring: HWANG Hae, YUN Jeong-hui, SHIN Il-ryong

Thieves in Love/Two Thieves in Love (Yeonae Dojeok)

1971 / 35mm / 108 min / original negative existing
Production Company: Anyang Films
Script: SHIN Sang-ok
Starring: Ling Yun, Twist KIM
Original negative kept at Korean Film Archive

War and Humanity/War and Human Being (Jeonjaeng-gwa Ingan)

1971 (Film no longer extant)
Running time or film specifics unknown
Production Company: Anyang Films
Script: GWAK Il-lo
Cinematography: SHIN Sang-ok
Lighting: MA Yong-cheon
Editing: KIM Hui-su
Music: HWANG Mun-pyeong
Starring: NAMGUNG Won, PARK No-sik, KIM So-ra

Lady of the Court/A Court Lady (Gungnyeo)

1972 / 35mm / 98 min / 2.35:1 / Color
Production Company: Anyang Films
Script: GWAK Il-lo
Cinematography: CHOE Seung-woo
Lighting: KIM Tae-seong
Editing: KIM Hyeon
Music: JEONG Yun-ju
Starring: YUN Jeong-hui, SHIN Yeong-gyun, PARK No-sik, JEON Yang-ja
Print stored at Korean Film Archive

Sim Cheong (Hyonyeo Simcheong)

1972 / 35mm / 120 min / 2.35:1 / Color
Production Company: Anyang Films
Script: LEE Sang-hyeon
Cinematography: CHOE Seung-woo
Lighting: MA Yong-cheon
Editing: KIM Hyeon

Music: JEONG Yun-ju
Starring: YUN Jeong-hui, KIM Seong-won, SHIN Sung-il, CHOI Eun-hee
Print stored at Korean Film Archive

The Three-Day Reign/Three Days of Their Reign (Samil Cheonha)

1973 / 35mm / 132 min / 2.35:1 / Color
Production Company: Anyang Films
Script: GWAK Il-lo
Cinematography: CHOE Seung-woo
Lighting: HAM Wan-seop
Editing: KIM Hyeon
Music: HWANG Mun-pyeong
Starring: SHIN Yeong-gyun, SHIN Sung-il, YUN Jeong-hui, PARK No-sik
Print stored at Korean Film Archive

Farewell (Ibyeol)

1973 / 35mm / 92 min / 2.35:1 / Color
Production Company: Anyang Films
Script: GWAK Il-lo
Cinematography: SHIN Sang-ok
Editing: HYEON Dong-chun
Music: HWANG Mun-pyeong
Starring: KIM Ji-mi, SHIN Sung-il, OH Su-mi, HAN Muk
Print stored at Korean Film Archive

Woman with Half a Soul/A Woman with Half Soul (Banhonnyeo)

1973 / 35mm / 90 min / 2.35:1 / Color
Production Company: Shin Productions
Script: YU Il-su, GWAK Il-lo
Cinematography: CHOE Seung-woo
Lighting: MA Yong-cheon
Music: JEONG Yun-ju
Starring: RI Ching, LEE Seung-yong, KIM Mu-yeong, JU Yeong
Print stored at Korean Film Archive

The Principal Visits Seoul (Gyojang Seonsaeng Sanggyeonggi)

1973 / 35mm / 98 min / 2.35:1 / Color
Production Company: Anyang Films
Script: SHIN Bong-seung
Cinematography: GANG Yong-nam
Starring: HEO Jang-gang, AHN In-suk, KIM Seong-won, NA O-mi
Print stored at Korean Film Archive

The Han River (Hangang)

1974 / 35mm / 97 min / 2.35:1 / Color
Production Company: Shin Productions
Script: LEE Sang-hyeon
Cinematography: CHOE Seung-woo
Lighting: MA Yong-cheon
Music: JEONG Yun-ju
Starring: CHOI Eun-hee, JANG Dong-hwi, PARK Am, SONG Mi-nam
Print stored at Korean Film Archive

At 13 Years Old/A Boy at His Age of 13 (13-se Sonyeon)

1974 / 35mm / 85 min / 2.35:1 / Color
Production Company: Shin Productions
Script: LEE Sang-hyeon, SHIN Sang-ok
Cinematography: CHOE Seung-woo
Starring: SHIN Sung-il, KIM Jeong-hun, NA Ha-yeong
Print stored at Korean Film Archive

I Love Mama

1975 / 35mm / 112 min / 2.35:1 / Color
Production Company: Shin Productions
Script: LEE Sang-hyeon
Cinematography: CHOE Seung-woo
Starring: CHOI Eun-hee, NAMGUNG Won, PARK Seong-gyu
Print stored at Korean Film Archive

The Rose and the Wild Dog/Rose and Wild Dog (Jangmi-wa Deulgae)

1975 / 35mm / 100 min / 2.35:1 / Color
Production Company: Habdong Production Company
Script: SHIN Sang-ok
Starring: OH Su-mi, DEUNG Rang-yeong, GEUM Bi, Chen Ko-tai
Print stored at Korean Film Archive

Chun-hie 75

1975 / 35mm / 90 min / 2.35:1 / Color
Production Company: Shin Productions
Script: YU Dong-hun, KIM Ha-rim

Cinematography: CHOE Seung-woo
Lighting: MA Yong-cheon
Editing: KIM Hyeon
Music: KIM Hui-gap
Starring: OH Su-mi, SHIN Jin-il, CHOE Nam-hyeon, LEE Il-woong
Print stored at Korean Film Archive

Prisoner 407/Woman Prisoner No. 407 (Yeosu 407)

1976 / 35mm / 94 min / 2.35:1 / Color
Production Company: Habdong Productions
Script: LEE Sang-hyeon
Cinematography: CHOE Gil-seon
Starring: HEO Jin, HO Pik-yu, SEO Mi-gyeong
Print stored at Korean Film Archive

Woman Prisoner No. 407 II (Yeosu 407 [Sok])

1976 / 35mm / 100 min / 2.35:1 / Color
Production Company: Habdong Productions
Script: LEE Sang-hyeon
Cinematography: CHOE Gil-seon
Starring: HEO Jin, HO Pik-yu, JIN Bong-jin
Print stored at Korean Film Archive

The Secret Envoy Who Never Returned (Doraoji Anhneun Milsa)

1984 / Shin Films Studio, North Korea

Oh My Love (Sarang Sarang Nae Sarang)

1984 / Shin Films Studio, North Korea

Escape Diary (Talchulgi)

1984 / Shin Films Studio, North Korea

Salt (Sogeum)

1985 / Shin Films Studio, North Korea

The Story of Simcheong (Simcheongjeon)

1985 / Shin Films Studio, North Korea

Breakwater (Bangpaje)

1985 / Shin Film Studio, North Korea

Pulgasari

1985 / Shin Films Studio, North Korea

Mayumi

1990 / 35mm / 110 min / 1.85:1 / Color
Production Company: Gil Films
Script: SHIN Bong-seung
Cinematography: Michael Lawler, John Coats, GU Jung-mo
Lighting: KIM Gang-il
Editing: KIM Hyeon
Music: GANG In-gu
Starring: KIM Seo-ra, LEE Hak-jae, SHIN Sung-il, George Kennedy
Print stored at Korean Film Archive

3 Ninjas Knuckle Up

1995 / 85 min
Production Company: Sheen Productions Inc.
Script: Alex S. Kim
Cinematography: Eugene D. Shlugleit
Music: Gary S. Scott
Editing: Pamela Choules
Starring: Max Elliott Slade, Victor Wong, Jeff Cadiente, Wayne Collins Jr., Gary Epper
International Distribution: Tristar Pictures

Evaporation/Vanished (Jeungbal)

1994 / 35mm / 115 min / 1.85:1 / Color
Production Company: Habdong Films
Script: Dasaka Akira, KIM Gang-yun, SHIN Sang-ok
Cinematography: PARK Seung-bae, Eugene D. Shlugleit
Lighting: KIM Gang-il, Louie Escobar
Editing: PARK Seong-bae, Scott Gamzon, Elliot Jacobson
Starring: KIM Hui-ra, SHIN Sung-il, George Takei, GANG Ri-na
Print stored at Korean Film Archive

A Winter Story (A Winter Story)

2004 / 35mm / 84 min / 1.85:1 / Color
(unreleased)
Starring: SHIN Koo, KIM Ji-sook, KIM Seon-dong, MUN Hyeok

About the Author

Yi Hyo-in

Yi Hyo-in is a professor in the Department of Theater & Film at Kyung Hee University and a film critic. He has served as Director of the Korean Film Archive, Executive Committee Chair for the Seoul Independent Film Festival, and Chief Director of the National Film Research Institute. He received his doctoral degree from Chung-Ang University for his dissertation *A Study of North Korean Films for the Creation of the "Great Leader" Image*, and he has published several books, including *A Sociocultural History of South Korea Read Through Film.*

Index